THE LETTERS OF SAINT PAUL
TO THE GALATIANS
AND
TO THE EPHESIANS

THE IGNATIUS CATHOLIC STUDY BIBLE

REVISED STANDARD VERSION
SECOND CATHOLIC EDITION

THE LETTERS OF SAINT PAUL
TO THE GALATIANS
AND
TO THE EPHESIANS

With Introduction, Commentary, and Notes

by

Scott Hahn and Curtis Mitch

and

with Study Questions by

Dennis Walters

IGNATIUS PRESS   SAN FRANCISCO

Published with ecclesiastical approval.

Original RSV Bible text:
Nihil obstat: Thomas Hanlon, S.T.L., L.S.S., Ph.L.
Imprimatur: +Peter W. Bertholome, D.D.
Bishop of Saint Cloud, Minnesota
May 11, 1966

Second Catholic Edition approved under the same *imprimatur* by the
Secretariat for Doctrine and Pastoral Practices,
National Conference of Catholic Bishops
February 29, 2000

Introduction, commentaries, and notes:
Nihil obstat: Rev. Msgr. J. Warren Holleran, S.T.D.
Imprimatur: + William J. Levada,
Archbishop of San Francisco,
May 26, 2005

The *nihil obstat* and *imprimatur* are official declarations that a book or pamphlet is free of doctrinal or moral error. No implication is contained therein that those who have granted the *nihil obstat* and *imprimatur* agree with the contents, opinions, or statements expressed.

Cover art:
The Leuville Epistles (16th century)
Heading of Chapter 1, St. Paul's Epistle to the Ephesians

Photo credit:
Victoria & Albert Museum, London / Art Resource, N.Y.

Cover design by Riz Boncan Marsella

Published by Ignatius Press, 2005
Bible text: Revised Standard Version, Second Catholic Edition
© 2005 by the Division of Christian Education of the
National Council of the Churches of Christ in the United States of America
All rights reserved

Introductions, commentaries, notes, headings, and study questions
© 2005 by Ignatius Press, San Francisco
All rights reserved
ISBN 978-1-58617-090-5
ISBN 1-58617-090-2
Printed in the United States of America ∞

CONTENTS

INTRODUCTION TO THE IGNATIUS STUDY BIBLE

You are approaching the "word of God". This is the title Christians most commonly give to the Bible, and the expression is rich in meaning. It is also the title given to the Second Person of the Blessed Trinity, God the Son. For Jesus Christ became flesh for our salvation, and "the name by which he is called is The Word of God" (Rev 19:13; cf. Jn 1:14).

The word of God is Scripture. The Word of God is Jesus. This close association between God's *written* word and his *eternal* Word is intentional and has been the custom of the Church since the first generation. "All Sacred Scripture is but one book, and this one book is Christ, 'because all divine Scripture speaks of Christ, and all divine Scripture is fulfilled in Christ'[1]" (CCC 134). This does not mean that the Scriptures are divine in the same way that Jesus is divine. They are, rather, divinely inspired and, as such, are unique in world literature, just as the Incarnation of the eternal Word is unique in human history.

Yet we can say that the inspired word resembles the incarnate Word in several important ways. Jesus Christ is the Word of God incarnate. In his humanity, he is like us in all things, except for sin. As a work of man, the Bible is like any other book, except without error. Both Christ and Scripture, says the Second Vatican Council, are given "for the sake of our salvation" (*Dei Verbum* 11), and both give us God's definitive revelation of himself. We cannot, therefore, conceive of one without the other: the Bible without Jesus, or Jesus without the Bible. Each is the interpretive key to the other. And because Christ is the subject of all the Scriptures, St. Jerome insists, "Ignorance of the Scriptures is ignorance of Christ"[2] (CCC 133).

When we approach the Bible, then, we approach Jesus, the Word of God; and in order to encounter Jesus, we must approach him in a prayerful study of the inspired word of God, the Sacred Scriptures.

Inspiration and Inerrancy The Catholic Church makes mighty claims for the Bible, and our acceptance of those claims is essential if we are to read the Scriptures and apply them to our lives as the Church intends. So it is not enough merely to nod at words like "inspired", "unique", or "inerrant". We have to understand what the Church means by these terms, and we have to make that understanding our own. After all, what we believe about the Bible will inevitably influence the way we read the Bible. The way we read the Bible, in turn, will determine what we "get out" of its sacred pages.

These principles hold true no matter what we read: a news report, a search warrant, an advertisement, a paycheck, a doctor's prescription, an eviction notice. How (or whether) we read these things depends largely upon our preconceived notions about the reliability and authority of their sources—and the potential they have for affecting our lives. In some cases, to misunderstand a document's authority can lead to dire consequences. In others, it can keep us from enjoying rewards that are rightfully ours. In the case of the Bible, both the rewards and the consequences involved take on an ultimate value.

What does the Church mean, then, when she affirms the words of St. Paul: "All Scripture is inspired by God" (2 Tim 3:16)? Since the term "inspired" in this passage could be translated "God-breathed", it follows that God breathed forth his word in the Scriptures as you and I breathe forth air when we speak. This means that God is the primary author of the Bible. He certainly employed human authors in this task as well, but he did not merely assist them while they wrote or subsequently approve what they had written. God the Holy Spirit is the *principal* author of Scripture, while the human writers are *instrumental* authors. These human authors freely wrote everything, and only those things, that God wanted: the word of God in the very words of God. This miracle of dual authorship extends to the whole of Scripture, and to every one of its parts, so that whatever the human authors affirm, God likewise affirms through their words.

The principle of biblical inerrancy follows logically from this principle of divine authorship. After all, God cannot lie, and he cannot make mistakes. Since the Bible is divinely inspired, it must be without error in everything that its divine and human authors affirm to be true. This means that biblical inerrancy is a mystery even broader in scope than infallibility, which guarantees for us that the Church will always teach the truth concerning faith and morals. Of course the mantle of inerrancy likewise covers faith and morals, but it extends even farther to ensure that all the facts and events of salvation history are accurately presented for us in the Scriptures. Inerrancy is our guarantee that the words and deeds of God found in the Bible are unified and true, declaring with one voice the wonders of his saving love.

---

[1] Hugh of St. Victor, *De arca Noe* 2, 8: PL 176, 642: cf. ibid. 2, 9: PL 176, 642–43.
[2] *DV* 25; cf. Phil 3:8 and St. Jerome, *Commentariorum Isaiam libri xviii*, prol.: PL 24, 17b.

The guarantee of inerrancy does not mean, however, that the Bible is an all-purpose encyclopedia of information covering every field of study. The Bible is not, for example, a textbook in the empirical sciences, and it should not be treated as one. When biblical authors relate facts of the natural order, we can be sure they are speaking in a purely descriptive and "phenomenological" way, according to the way things appeared to their senses.

Biblical Authority Implicit in these doctrines is God's desire to make himself known to the world and to enter a loving relationship with every man, woman, and child he has created. God gave us the Scriptures not just to inform or motivate us; more than anything he wants to save us. This higher purpose underlies every page of the Bible, indeed every word of it.

In order to reveal himself, God used what theologians call "accommodation". Sometimes the Lord stoops down to communicate by "condescension"—that is, he speaks as humans speak, as if he had the same passions and weakness that we do (for example, God says he was "sorry" that he made man in Genesis 6:6). Other times he communicates by "elevation"—that is, by endowing human words with divine power (for example, through the prophets). The numerous examples of divine accommodation in the Bible are an expression of God's wise and fatherly ways. For a sensitive father can speak with his children either by condescension, as in baby talk, or by elevation, by bringing a child's understanding up to a more mature level.

God's word is thus saving, fatherly, and personal. Because it speaks directly to us, we must never be indifferent to its content; after all, the word of God is at once the object, cause, and support of our faith. It is, in fact, a test of our faith, since we see in the Scriptures only what faith disposes us to see. If we believe what the Church believes, we will see in Scripture the saving, inerrant, and divinely authored revelation of the Father. If we believe otherwise, we see another book altogether.

This test applies not only to rank-and-file believers but also to the Church's theologians and hierarchy, and even the Magisterium. Vatican II has stressed in recent times that Scripture must be "the very soul of sacred theology" (*Dei Verbum* 24). Pope Benedict XVI echoes this powerful teaching with his own, insisting that, "The *normative theologians* are the authors of Holy Scripture" [emphasis added]. Elsewhere he reminds us that Scripture and the Church's dogmatic teaching are tied tightly together, to the point of being inseparable. He states: "Dogma is by definition nothing other than an interpretation of Scripture." The defined dogmas of our faith, then, encapsulate the Church's infallible interpretation of Scripture, and theology is a further reflection upon that work.

The Senses of Scripture Because the Bible has both divine and human authors, we are required to master a different sort of reading than we are used to. First, we must read Scripture according to its *literal* sense, as we read any other human literature. At this initial stage, we strive to discover the meaning of the words and expressions used by the biblical writers as they were understood in their original setting and by their original recipients. This means, among other things, that we do not interpret everything we read "literalistically", as though Scripture never speaks in a figurative or symbolic way (it often does!). Rather, we read it according to the rules that govern its different literary forms of writing, depending on whether we are reading a narrative, a poem, a letter, a parable, or an apocalyptic vision. The Church calls us to read the divine books in this way to ensure that we understand what the human authors were laboring to explain to God's people.

The literal sense, however, is not the only sense of Scripture, since we interpret its sacred pages according to the *spiritual* senses as well. In this way, we search out what the Holy Spirit is trying to tell us, beyond even what the human authors have consciously asserted. Whereas the literal sense of Scripture describes a historical reality—a fact, precept, or event—the spiritual senses disclose deeper mysteries revealed through the historical realities. What the soul is to the body, the spiritual senses are to the literal. You can distinguish them; but if you try to separate them, death immediately follows. St. Paul was the first to insist upon this and warn of its consequences: "God . . . has qualified us to be ministers of a new covenant, not in a written code but in the Spirit; for the written code kills, but the Spirit gives life" (2 Cor 3:5–6).

Catholic tradition recognizes three spiritual senses that stand upon the foundation of the literal sense of Scripture (see CCC 115). (1) The first is the *allegorical* sense, which unveils the spiritual and prophetic meaning of biblical history. Allegorical interpretations thus reveal how persons, events, and institutions of Scripture can point beyond themselves toward greater mysteries yet to come (OT), or display the fruits of mysteries already revealed (NT). Christians have often read the Old Testament in this way to discover how the mystery of Christ in the New Covenant was once hidden in the Old, and how the full significance of the Old Covenant was finally made manifest in the New. Allegorical significance is likewise latent in the New Testament, especially in the life and deeds of Jesus recorded in the Gospels. Because Christ is the Head of the Church and the source of her spiritual life, what was accomplished in Christ the Head during his earthly life prefigures what he continually produces in his members through grace. The allegorical sense builds up the virtue of faith. (2) The second is the *tropological* or *moral* sense, which

reveals how the actions of God's people in the Old Testament and the life of Jesus in the New Testament prompt us to form virtuous habits in our own lives. It therefore draws from Scripture warnings against sin and vice, as well as inspirations to pursue holiness and purity. The moral sense is intended to build up the virtue of charity. (3) The third is the *anagogical* sense, which points upward to heavenly glory. It shows us how countless events in the Bible prefigure our final union with God in eternity, and how things that are "seen" on earth are figures of things "unseen" in heaven. Because the anagogical sense leads us to contemplate our destiny, it is meant to build up the virtue of hope. Together with the literal sense, then, these spiritual senses draw out the fullness of what God wants to give us through his Word and as such comprise what ancient tradition has called the "full sense" of Sacred Scripture.

All of this means that the deeds and events of the Bible are charged with meaning beyond what is immediately apparent to the reader. In essence, that meaning is Jesus Christ and the salvation he died to give us. This is especially true of the books of the New Testament, which proclaim Jesus explicitly; but it is also true of the Old Testament, which speaks of Jesus in more hidden and symbolic ways. The human authors of the Old Testament told us as much as they were able, but they could not clearly discern the shape of all future events standing at such a distance. It is the Bible's divine Author, the Holy Spirit, who could and did foretell the saving work of Christ, from the first page of the Book of Genesis onward.

The New Testament did not, therefore, abolish the Old. Rather, the New fulfilled the Old, and in doing so, it lifted the veil that kept hidden the face of the Lord's bride. Once the veil is removed, we suddenly see the world of the Old Covenant charged with grandeur. Water, fire, clouds, gardens, trees, hills, doves, lambs—all of these things are memorable details in the history and poetry of Israel. But now, seen in the light of Jesus Christ, they are much more. For the Christian with eyes to see, water symbolizes the saving power of Baptism; fire, the Holy Spirit; the spotless lamb, Christ crucified; Jerusalem, the city of heavenly glory.

The spiritual reading of Scripture is nothing new. Indeed the very first Christians read the Bible this way. St. Paul describes Adam as a "type" that prefigured Jesus Christ (Rom 5:14). A "type" is a real person, place, thing, or event in the Old Testament that foreshadows something greater in the New. From this term we get the word "typology", referring to the study of how the Old Testament prefigures Christ (CCC 128–30). Elsewhere St. Paul draws deeper meanings out of the story of Abraham's sons, declaring, "This is an allegory" (Gal 4:24). He is not suggesting that these events of the distant past never really happened; he is saying that the events both happened *and* signified something more glorious yet to come.

The New Testament later describes the Tabernacle of ancient Israel as "a copy and shadow of the heavenly sanctuary" (Heb 8:5) and the Mosaic Law as a "shadow of the good things to come" (Heb 10:1). St. Peter, in turn, notes that Noah and his family were "saved through water" in a way that "corresponds" to sacramental Baptism, which "now saves you" (1 Pet 3:20–21). Interestingly, the expression that is translated "corresponds" in this verse is a Greek term that denotes the fulfillment or counterpart of an ancient "type".

We need not look to the apostles, however, to justify a spiritual reading of the Bible. After all, Jesus himself read the Old Testament this way. He referred to Jonah (Mt 12:39), Solomon (Mt 12:42), the Temple (Jn 2:19), and the brazen serpent (Jn 3:14) as "signs" that pointed forward to him. We see in Luke's Gospel, as Christ comforted the disciples on the road to Emmaus, that "beginning with Moses and all the prophets, he interpreted to them in all the Scriptures the things concerning himself" (Lk 24:27). It was precisely this extensive spiritual interpretation of the Old Testament that made such an impact on these once-discouraged travelers, causing their hearts to "burn" within them (Lk 24:32).

Criteria for Biblical Interpretation We too must learn to discern the "full sense" of Scripture as it includes both the literal and spiritual senses together. Still, this does not mean we should "read into" the Bible meanings that are not really there. Spiritual exegesis is not an unrestrained flight of the imagination. Rather, it is a sacred science that proceeds according to certain principles and stands accountable to sacred tradition, the Magisterium, and the wider community of biblical interpreters (both living and deceased).

In searching out the full sense of a text, we should always avoid the extreme tendency to "over-spiritualize" in a way that minimizes or denies the Bible's literal truth. St. Thomas Aquinas was well aware of this danger and asserted that "all other senses of Sacred Scripture are based on the literal" (*STh* I, 1, 10, *ad* 1, quoted in CCC 116). On the other hand, we should never confine the meaning of a text to the literal, intended sense of its human author, as if the divine Author did not intend the passage to be read in the light of Christ's coming.

Fortunately the Church has given us guidelines in our study of Scripture. The unique character and divine authorship of the Bible calls us to read it "in the Spirit" (*Dei Verbum* 12). Vatican II outlines this teaching in a practical way by directing us to read the Scriptures according to three specific criteria:

1. We must "[b]e especially attentive 'to the content and unity of the whole Scripture'" (CCC 112).

2. We must "[r]ead the Scripture within 'the living Tradition of the whole Church' " (CCC 113).

3. We must "[b]e attentive to the analogy of faith" (CCC 114; cf. Rom 12:6).

These criteria protect us from many of the dangers that ensnare readers of the Bible, from the newest inquirer to the most prestigious scholar. Reading Scripture out of context is one such pitfall, and probably the one most difficult to avoid. A memorable cartoon from the 1950s shows a young man poring over the pages of the Bible. He says to his sister: "Don't bother me now; I'm trying to find a Scripture verse to back up one of my preconceived notions." No doubt a biblical text pried from its context can be twisted to say something very different from what its author actually intended.

The Church's criteria guide us here by defining what constitutes the authentic "context" of a given biblical passage. The first criterion directs us to the literary context of every verse, including not only the words and paragraphs that surround it, but also the entire corpus of the biblical author's writings and, indeed, the span of the entire Bible. The *complete* literary context of any Scripture verse includes every text from Genesis to Revelation—because the Bible is a unified book, not just a library of different books. When the Church canonized the Book of Revelation, for example, she recognized it to be incomprehensible apart from the wider context of the entire Bible.

The second criterion places the Bible firmly within the context of a community that treasures a "living tradition". That community is the People of God down through the ages. Christians lived out their faith for well over a millennium before the printing press was invented. For centuries, few believers owned copies of the Gospels, and few people could read anyway. Yet they absorbed the gospel—through the sermons of their bishops and clergy, through prayer and meditation, through Christian art, through liturgical celebrations, and through oral tradition. These were expressions of the one "living tradition", a culture of living faith that stretches from ancient Israel to the contemporary Church. For the early Christians, the gospel could not be understood apart from that tradition. So it is with us. Reverence for the Church's tradition is what protects us from any sort of chronological or cultural provincialism, such as scholarly fads that arise and carry away a generation of interpreters before being dismissed by the next generation.

The third criterion places scriptural texts within the framework of faith. If we believe that the Scriptures are divinely inspired, we must also believe them to be internally coherent and consistent with all the doctrines that Christians believe. Remember, the Church's dogmas (such as the Real Presence, the papacy, the Immaculate Conception) are not something *added* to Scripture, but are the Church's infallible interpretation *of* Scripture.

Using This Study Guide This volume is designed to lead the reader through Scripture according to the Church's guidelines—faithful to the canon, to the tradition, and to the creeds. The Church's interpretive principles have thus shaped the component parts of this book, and they are designed to make the reader's study as effective and rewarding as possible.

Introductions: We have introduced the biblical book with an essay covering issues such as authorship, date of composition, purpose, and leading themes. This background information will assist readers to approach and understand the text on its own terms.

Annotations: The basic notes at the bottom of every page help the user to read the Scriptures with understanding. They by no means exhaust the meaning of the sacred text but provide background material to help the reader make sense of what he reads. Often these notes make explicit what the sacred writers assumed or held to be implicit. They also provide scores of historical, cultural, geographical, and theological information pertinent to the inspired narratives—information that can help the reader bridge the distance between the biblical world and his own.

Cross-References: Between the biblical text at the top of each page and the annotations at the bottom, numerous references are listed to point readers to other scriptural passages related to the one being studied. This follow-up is an essential part of any serious study. It is also an excellent way to discover how the content of Scripture "hangs together" in a providential unity. Along with biblical cross-references, the annotations refer to select paragraphs from the *Catechism of the Catholic Church*. These are not doctrinal "proof texts" but are designed to help the reader interpret the Bible in accordance with the mind of the Church. The *Catechism* references listed either handle the biblical text directly or treat a broader doctrinal theme that sheds significant light on that text.

Topical Essays, Word Studies, Charts: These features bring readers to a deeper understanding of select details. The *topical essays* take up major themes and explain them more thoroughly and theologically than the annotations, often relating them to the doctrines of the Church. Occasionally the annotations are supplemented by *word studies* that put readers in touch with the ancient languages of Scripture. These should help readers to understand better and appreciate the inspired terminology that runs throughout the sacred books. Also included are various *charts* that summarize biblical information "at a glance".

Icon Annotations: Three distinctive icons are

interspersed throughout the annotations, each one corresponding to one of the Church's three criteria for biblical interpretation. Bullets indicate the passage or passages to which these icons apply.

Notes marked by the book icon relate to the "content and unity" of Scripture, showing how particular passages of the Old Testament illuminate the mysteries of the New. Much of the information in these notes explains the original context of the citations and indicates how and why this has a direct bearing on Christ or the Church. Through these notes, the reader can develop a sensitivity to the beauty and unity of God's saving plan as it stretches across both Testaments.

Notes marked by the dove icon examine particular passages in light of the Church's "living tradition". Because the Holy Spirit both guides the Magisterium and inspires the spiritual senses of Scripture, these annotations supply information along both of these lines. On the one hand, they refer to the Church's doctrinal teaching as presented by various popes, creeds, and ecumenical councils; on the other, they draw from (and paraphrase) the spiritual interpretations of various Fathers, Doctors, and saints.

Notes marked by the keys icon pertain to the "analogy of faith". Here we spell out how the mysteries of our faith "unlock" and explain one another. This type of comparison between Christian beliefs displays the coherence and unity of defined dogmas, which are the Church's infallible interpretations of Scripture.

Putting It All in Perspective Perhaps the most important context of all we have saved for last: the interior life of the individual reader. What we get out of the Bible will largely depend on how we approach the Bible. Unless we are living a sustained and disciplined life of prayer, we will never have the reverence, the profound humility, or the grace we need to see the Scriptures for what they really are.

You are approaching the "word of God". But for thousands of years, since before he knit you in your mother's womb, the Word of God has been approaching you.

One Final Note. The volume you hold in your hands is only a small part of a much larger work still in production. Study helps similar to those printed in this booklet are being prepared for *all* the books of the Bible and will appear gradually as they are finished. Our ultimate goal is to publish a single, one-volume Study Bible that will include the entire text of Scripture, along with all the annotations, charts, cross-references, maps, and other features found in the following pages. Individual booklets will be published in the meantime, with the hope that God's people can begin to benefit from this labor before its full completion.

We have included a long list of Study Questions in the back to make this format as useful as possible, not only for individual study but for group settings and discussions as well. The questions are designed to help readers both "understand" the Bible and "apply" it to their lives. We pray that God will make use of our efforts and yours to help renew the face of the earth! «

INTRODUCTION TO THE
LETTER OF SAINT PAUL TO THE GALATIANS

Author and Date The opening line of Galatians identifies its author as the Apostle Paul (1:1). With the exception of a few skeptical opinions in modern times, this claim has never been seriously contested. The early Church held this view unanimously, and the contents of the letter, theological and autobiographical, confirm beyond a reasonable doubt that Paul must have written it as he said (6:11).

Dating the composition of the letter is more difficult. The question hinges in part on the identity of Paul's addressees: the "churches of Galatia" (1:2). If the apostle is writing to the churches of South Galatia that he established on his first missionary journey (Acts 14:1–23), then he could have penned the epistle as early as A.D. 48. But if Paul addresses churches in North Galatia that he seems to have founded on his second missionary journey (Acts 16:6), then he could not have written the letter before A.D. 50. These differing dates mean that Paul's visit to Jerusalem mentioned in 2:1–10 is an important factor that must be considered. Those who prefer the earlier date contend that Paul is referring in these verses to the visit to Judea mentioned in Acts 11:29–30. Those who prefer a later date suggest that Paul is describing the Jerusalem Council of Acts 15:1–29, which convened in A.D. 49. On balance, the evidence leans in favor of a later date over an earlier one. Several parallels between Paul's comments in 2:1–10 and the circumstances of the Jerusalem Council suggest that Paul is looking back on this important event (see note on 2:1–10). Galatians, therefore, was probably written in the early or mid 50s.

Destination The Roman Province of Galatia was established in 25 B.C. in the central territory of Asia Minor (modern Turkey). Prior to this, migrant tribes from Gaul had settled in the northern parts of this territory in the third century B.C. and were long known as the "Galatians". This has made it exceedingly difficult for scholars to identify the Christians whom Paul was addressing by that name (3:1). Many argue that Paul's letter was written solely for these northern Galatians, since Greco-Roman sources use the title "Galatians" as a purely *ethnic* reference to these tribal immigrants. Others contend that in the NT period, "Galatians" could also be used as a *territorial* reference to anyone living within the boundaries of the province, regardless of whether they lived in the northern or southern regions. The Jewish historian Josephus seems to use it in this more general way. Thus, with the term "Galatians" becoming more inclusive by

the first century—at least in Paul's Jewish environment—it is nearly impossible to favor one view over another merely on the basis of the name (3:1). Until decisive evidence surfaces, we can be sure only that Paul was addressing Christians who lived somewhere in the province of Galatia, even though the question of North or South Galatia remains an open one.

Purpose Paul wrote this letter to defend his gospel against opponents and to dissuade the Galatians from receiving circumcision. Apparently rival missionaries, known as Judaizers, infiltrated the ranks of the Galatian churches during Paul's absence and stirred up trouble among his Gentile converts. Internal evidence within the letter suggests they preached a false gospel (1:6–7) that pressured Gentile Christians to embrace circumcision and the ceremonial laws of the Old Covenant as indispensable requirements for salvation (5:2–12; 6:12–13). Although they professed to be Christians, they felt that Paul's gospel of "faith working through love" (5:6) was incomplete without the ritual observances of the Mosaic Law. The success that these Judaizers enjoyed in Galatia forced Paul to respond with a vigorous defense of the gospel (1:11–2:10) and a sophisticated explanation of how the New Covenant inaugurated by Christ dispenses with the ceremonies of the Old (chaps. 3–4). In his view, to add circumcision and other Mosaic requirements to the gospel is to exchange freedom in Christ for spiritual slavery (2:4; 5:1). Stern warnings thus punctuate this letter as Paul appeals to the Galatians to distance themselves from the Judaizers and to disregard their propaganda.

Themes and Characteristics Galatians is clearly the most polemical of Paul's letters. Although it shares much in common with the more formal Letter to the Romans, the apologetic tone of this letter is heated and, at times, even combative. There can be no question that Paul perceived the Galatian crisis as a great spiritual threat to everyone involved. As he saw it, the issues at stake touched the very heart of Christian identity and demanded a forceful defense of the gospel.

What was the essence of this controversy, and why was it so important for Paul to resolve it quickly and decisively? For the most part, Galatians is Paul's attempt to define the essence of the New Covenant in Christ over against the Old Covenant that gave birth to it. This is why circumcision is the towering issue of the letter, with the Judaizers

promoting it, Paul attacking it, and the Galatians caught in the crossfire. Before the coming of Christ, the rite of circumcision was the doorway into God's covenant with Abraham (Gen 17:9–14) and the sacrament of initiation into the family of Israel (Lev 12:3). The Crucifixion of Jesus Christ, however, marks a turning point in covenant history where circumcision is now set aside, along with the entire body of liturgical and ceremonial legislation promulgated by Moses. Through his Cross, Christ has redeemed us from the curses of the Old Covenant (3:13) and unleashed the divine blessings of the New Covenant in a powerful way, inaugurating a "new creation" (6:15) and a renewed "Israel" (6:16). As Paul shows from the Scriptures, the New Covenant ratified by Christ *fulfills* the Abrahamic covenant of blessing for all nations even as it *terminates* the Mosaic covenant that was confined to the one nation of Israel in the centuries between Abraham and Christ. Now, whoever embraces Christ in faith (3:7) and receives Baptism (3:27) becomes a spiritual descendant of Abraham and an adopted child of God (4:1–7).

Paul's effort in this letter to define the terms of the gospel has made Galatians one of his most important writings. Although storms of controversy have continued to gather around this epistle throughout the centuries, we would be greatly impoverished without it. Galatians still stands as a thunderous defense of the good news, reaffirming for all time that salvation comes only by grace through faith in the Lord Jesus Christ.

OUTLINE OF THE LETTER OF SAINT PAUL TO THE GALATIANS

1. **Opening Address (1:1-9)**
   A. Salutation (1:1–5)
   B. Condemnation of False Gospels (1:6–9)

2. **Paul's Apostolic Authority (1:10—2:21)**
   A. Paul's Background and Divine Vocation (1:10–17)
   B. First Visit to Jerusalem (1:18–24)
   C. Second Visit to Jerusalem (2:1–10)
   D. Confrontation with Peter at Antioch (2:11–21)

3. **Paul's Apostolic Gospel (3:1—4:31)**
   A. Appeal to Galatian Experience (3:1–5)
   B. Faith and the Sons of Abraham (3:6–9)
   C. Covenant Curses and Covenant Promises (3:10–18)
   D. Purpose of the Law (3:19–29)
   E. Divine Adoption in Christ (4:1–7)
   F. Personal Appeal (4:8–20)
   G. Allegory of Sarah and Hagar (4:21–31)

4. **Christian Life and Liberty (5:1—6:10)**
   A. Freedom in Jesus Christ (5:1–15)
   B. Life in the Spirit (5:16–26)
   C. Life in the Household of Faith (6:1–10)

5. **Conclusion (6:11–18)**

Destinations for the travels of Saint Paul, including Galatia and Ephesus.

THE LETTER OF SAINT PAUL TO THE

GALATIANS

Salutation

1 Paul an apostle—not from men nor through man, but through Jesus Christ and God the Father, who raised him from the dead—²and all the brethren who are with me,

To the churches of Galatia:

3 Grace to you and peace from God the Father and our Lord Jesus Christ, ⁴who gave himself for our sins to deliver us from the present evil age, according to the will of our God and Father; ⁵to whom be the glory for ever and ever. Amen.

There Is No Other Gospel

6 I am astonished that you are so quickly deserting him who called you in the grace of Christ and turning to a different gospel— ⁷not that there is another gospel, but there are some who trouble you and want to pervert the gospel of Christ. ⁸But even if we, or an angel from heaven, should preach to you a gospel contrary to that which we preached to you, let him be accursed. ⁹As we have said before, so now I say again, If any one is preaching to you a gospel contrary to that which you received, let him be accursed.

10 Am I now seeking the favor of men, or of God? Or am I trying to please men? If I were still pleasing men, I should not be a servant ᵃ of Christ.

Paul's Vindication of His Apostleship

11 Brethren, I would have you know that the gospel which was preached by me is not man's ᵇ gospel. ¹²For I did not receive it from man, nor was I taught it, but it came through a revelation of Jesus Christ. ¹³For you have heard of my former

---

1.3. Rom 1.7.   **1.4.** Gal 2.20; 1 Tim 2:6.   **1:5:** Rom 16:27.   **1:8:** 2 Cor 11:4.
1:10: 1 Thess 2:4.   **1:11:** Rom 1:16–17.   **1:13:** Acts 8:3.

1:1–9 Unlike most Pauline letters, Galatians omits introductory expressions of praise and thanksgiving. Instead of his usual warmth, Paul opens with a sharp and confrontational tone, followed by an astonished rebuke (1:6–9). This tension is present throughout the epistle and comes to the surface in its many warnings (3:1; 4:11, 20; 5:1–12, 15; 6:7–9).

1:1 Paul an apostle: From the outset Paul defends his apostleship. Because his opponents in Galatia apparently denied him authority on a par with the Twelve, he contends that his commission stems neither from human authority (**from men**) nor even from the original apostles (**through man**). Paul, like the Twelve, received his gospel directly from Jesus Christ (1:12; Acts 26:15–18; CCC 659).

1:2 all the brethren: Not co-authors, but a group of fellow Christian supporters. **the churches:** Galatians is a circular letter directed to several congregations affected by the Judaizing crisis. It is disputed whether Paul was writing to those of North or South Galatia. See introduction: *Destination.*

1:3 Grace to you and peace: A conventional Pauline greeting (Rom 1:7; 1 Cor 1:3; 2 Cor 1:2).

1:4 gave himself for our sins: Anticipates the description of Christ's act of redemption in 3:13–14. Here and elsewhere Paul emphasizes that Jesus willingly offered himself as a sacrifice for our salvation (2:20; Eph 5:2; CCC 2824). **the present evil age:** Jewish theology distinguished between "this age", which is dominated by sin and death, and the "age to come" (Mt 12:32; Eph 1:21), when peace comes to reign in the cosmos and the powers of darkness are destroyed. Through Christ, the graces of the age to come are already pouring into the lives of believers, rescuing them from sin, selfishness, and Satan.

1:6 I am astonished: Paul is distressed that his readers have been so easily lured into error by false teachers (3:1). His concern for the integrity of the gospel is manifest through the severity of his language. **him who called you:** God, through the mediating grace of Christ (1:15; Rom 8:30). **a different gospel:** I.e., a false gospel at variance with Paul's apostolic teaching.

1:7 some who trouble you: The Judaizers, who labored to bring the Galatians under the yoke of circumcision and other burdensome laws of the Old Covenant (6:12–13). In doing so, they promoted a false gospel that implicitly denied the sufficiency of Christ's death for our salvation (2:21). Although our knowledge about these troublemakers is fragmentary, they seem to share the outlook and aims of Jewish traditionalists from Judea (Acts 15:1–5; 21:20–21).

1:10 trying to please men?: It seems Paul was accused of subtracting circumcision from the requirements of Christian initiation in order to please the Gentiles. Ironically, it is the Judaizers who are the real men-pleasers, since they preach circumcision in order to avoid persecution by their Jewish kinsmen (6:12). Paul's willingness to preach the true gospel in the face of persecution is evidence that he seeks only the approval of God (5:11; Acts 14:19–22).

1:12 through a revelation: Paul received his gospel directly from Christ, independent of apostolic tradition and instruction (Acts 26:12–18; CCC 153, 442). It is thus impossible that his message would conflict with that of the Jerusalem apostles who were also instructed by Christ, and in any case Paul has verified it with them (2:2; Acts 15:2). Notice that Paul is focusing on the foundational message of faith and salvation in Christ; other things, such as creeds and liturgical traditions, were indeed passed along to him by others (1 Cor 11:23–26; 15:3–7).

1:13 I persecuted the Church: A dark chapter in Paul's pre-Christian life, of which he was later ashamed (1 Cor 15:9; 1 Tim 1:13). His zeal for traditional Judaism spurred him to adopt violent and aggressive tactics that included harassing, imprisoning, and even executing early Christians (Acts 8:1–3; 9:1–2; 26:9–11). After his conversion, Paul's fiery enthusiasm was not lessened but given new direction by Christ.

ᵃ Or *slave.*
ᵇ Greek *according to man.*

life in Judaism, how I persecuted the Church of God violently and tried to destroy it; ¹⁴and I advanced in Judaism beyond many of my own age among my people, so extremely zealous was I for the traditions of my fathers. ¹⁵But when he who had set me apart before I was born, and had called me through his grace, ¹⁶was pleased to reveal his Son to ᶜ me, in order that I might preach him among the Gentiles, I did not confer with flesh and blood, ¹⁷nor did I go up to Jerusalem to those who were apostles before me, but I went away into Arabia; and again I returned to Damascus.

18 Then after three years I went up to Jerusalem to visit Ce′phas, and remained with him fifteen days. ¹⁹But I saw none of the other apostles except James the Lord's brother. ²⁰(In what I am writing to you, before God, I do not lie!) ²¹Then I went into the regions of Syria and Cili′cia. ²²And I was still not known by sight to the churches of Christ in Judea; ²³they only heard it said, "He who once persecuted us is now preaching the faith he once tried to destroy." ²⁴And they glorified God because of me.

Paul and the Other Apostles

2 Then after fourteen years I went up again to Jerusalem with Barnabas, taking Titus along with me. ²I went up by revelation; and I laid before

---

1:14: Acts 22:3.　　**1:15:** Acts 9:1–19; Is 49:1; Jer 1:5.　　**1:18:** Acts 9:26–30; 11:30.　　**2:1:** Acts 15:2.

1:14 traditions of my fathers: I.e., everything that comprised the Jewish way of life. This included biblical customs and institutions as well as Pharisaic practices that were devised to supplement and intensify the demands of the written Law (Mk 7:1–5). Paul studied under the famed Rabbi Gamaliel (Acts 22:3) and prided himself on a strict adherence to Jewish law (Phil 3:6).

1:15 set me apart: Paul's apostolic mission was predetermined before his birth. ● His language recalls Is 49:1 and Jer 1:5, where the messianic Servant and the prophet Jeremiah were consecrated before birth to be God's messengers. Paul's similar calling places him within this prophetic tradition.

1:16 to reveal his Son: In a vision on the road to Damascus (Acts 9:3–9; 1 Cor 9:1). It was then that Christ commissioned Paul to announce the gospel to the Gentiles and the sons of Israel (Acts 9:15–16). **I did not confer:** The RSV leaves the adverb "immediately" (Gk. *eutheōs*) untranslated. Paul does not deny that he consulted the original apostles about his gospel (2:2, 6–10); he simply underscores that his *certainty* about

ᶜ Greek *in*.

Word Study

Accursed (Gal 1:8)

Anathema (Gk.): "under a divine curse" or "set apart for destruction". The word is used six times in the NT, twice in Galatians. In the Greek OT, this word often translates a cultic and military term (Heb. *herem*) for the sacred ban that Yahweh placed on the enemy peoples of Canaan. Cities anathematized by the Lord were destined for utter destruction (Deut 20:17), and oftentimes the Israelites were forbidden to confiscate any booty for themselves (Deut 7:26; Josh 6:18). The same anathema was pronounced on cities where false prophets dared to lead God's people astray (Deut 13:12–18). The NT uses this term for a conditional curse that a person invokes upon himself when he swears an oath; it is a curse that will be activated if and when the individual breaks the oath (Acts 23:12–14). In Paul, an anathema is a curse that no Spirit-filled believer can invoke upon Jesus (1 Cor 12:3), yet it is precisely the divine judgment that awaits those who refuse to love the Lord (1 Cor 16:22). In Galatians, Paul pronounces an anathema upon heretical teachers who promote a false gospel. For the Hebrew background, see word study: *Devoted* at Josh 6:17.

---

its truth exempted him from the need to do so immediately after his conversion. **flesh and blood:** A Semitic idiom meaning "human beings" (Sir 14:18; Mt 16:17).

1:17 Arabia: Probably the territory of the Nabatean kingdom that stretched from Damascus, north of Palestine, down to the Red Sea, south of Palestine. This was mostly a wilderness region where no one could have instructed Paul but God himself. ● The reference to Arabia here and in 4:25 might suggest that Paul journeyed to the traditional site of Mt. Sinai (also called Horeb), where Moses and Elijah spoke intimately with the Lord (Ex 19:2–3; 1 Kings 19:8–18).

1:18 after three years: Corresponds to the "many days" that passed before Paul was forced to flee Damascus (Acts 9:23–25). It was then that he traveled to Jerusalem for the first time as a Christian (Acts 9:26–29). **to visit:** The Greek expression is more precise, indicating that Paul "interviewed" Peter as well as "made his acquaintance". He must have spent these two weeks gathering information about the life and ministry of Jesus. **Cephas:** Another name for Simon Peter, often used in Paul's letters (2:9, 11; 1 Cor 1:12; 9:5; 15:5). It transliterates an Aramaic word meaning "rock". See word study: *Peter* at Mt 16:18.

1:19 James: Tradition reveres James as the first bishop of Jerusalem, being appointed to this position by the apostles. Early Christians called him "the Just" on account of his disciplined, prayerful, and virtuous life (Eusebius, *Ecclesiastical History* 2, 23; St. Jerome, *On Illustrious Men* 2). See note on Acts 12:17. **the Lord's brother:** Not a blood brother, but a near kinsman (CCC 500). See note on Mt 12:46.

1:20 before God, I do not lie: A mild oath formula, sworn by Paul to insist on the reliability of his testimony (Rom 9:1; CCC 2154).

1:21 Syria and Cilicia: Paul withdrew first to his native city of Tarsus in Cilicia (Acts 9:30) and was later summoned to the Church of Antioch in Syria (Acts 11:25–26).

2:1–10 Scholars disagree over the precise circumstances of this Jerusalem visit. Some link it with the trip that Paul and Barnabas made to provide famine relief for the Judean Christians in Acts 11:28–30. More probably, Paul is referring to his presence at the Jerusalem Council in Acts 15:1–29. Notice that the two accounts concern (1) the same people (Paul, Barnabas, and companions, Acts 15:2), (2) the same place (Jerusalem, Acts 15:4), (3) the same leaders (Peter and James, Acts 15:7, 13), (4) the same issue (circumcision, Acts 15:1), and (5) the same opponents (the circumcision party, Acts 15:5).

2:1 after fourteen years: Probably calculated from the time of Paul's first visit to Jerusalem (1:18). **Barnabas:** A Levite and native of Cyprus. See note on Acts 4:36. **Titus:** One of Paul's trusted companions (2 Cor 2:13; Tit 1:4). He is mentioned here to illustrate that, although Titus was an uncircumcised Gentile, the Jerusalem apostles welcomed him into their fellowship (2:3).

2:2 I laid before them: Paul received his gospel directly from Christ (1:12), yet he submitted it for approval to the senior apostles in Jerusalem (Acts 15:2). This was to confirm that his

them (but privately before those who were of repute) the gospel which I preach among the Gentiles, lest somehow I should be running or had run in vain. [3]But even Titus, who was with me, was not compelled to be circumcised, though he was a Greek. [4]But because of false brethren secretly brought in, who slipped in to spy out our freedom which we have in Christ Jesus, that they might bring us into bondage—[5]to them we did not yield submission even for a moment, that the truth of the gospel might be preserved for you. [6]And from those who were reputed to be something (what they were makes no difference to me; God shows no partiality)—those, I say, who were of repute added nothing to me; [7]but on the contrary, when they saw that I had been entrusted with the gospel to the uncircumcised, just as Peter had been entrusted with the gospel to the circumcised [8](for he who worked through Peter for the mission to the circumcised worked through me also for the Gentiles), [9]and when they perceived the grace that was given to me, James and Ce′phas and John, who were reputed to be pillars, gave to me and Barnabas the right hand of fellowship, that we should go to the Gentiles and they to the circumcised; [10]only they would have us remember the poor, which very thing I was eager to do.

Paul Rebukes Peter at Antioch

11 But when Ce′phas came to Antioch I opposed him to his face, because he stood condemned. [12]For before certain men came from James, he ate with the Gentiles; but when they came he drew back and separated himself, fearing the circumcision party. [13]And with him the rest of the Jews acted insincerely, so that even Barnabas was carried away by their insincerity. [14]But when I saw that they were not straightforward about the truth of the gospel, I said to Ce′phas before them all, "If you, though a Jew, live like a Gentile and not like a Jew, how can you compel the Gentiles to live like Jews?" [15]We ourselves, who are Jews by birth and not Gentile sinners, [16]yet who know that a man is not justified [d]

2:5: Acts 15:23–29.   **2:6:** Deut 10:17.   **2:11:** Acts 11:19–26.   **2:16:** Ps 143:2; Rom 3:20.

---

message was in line with the doctrine of the Twelve and to remove suspicions that his missionary efforts were at odds with the authority of the Church's recognized leaders. In the end, the pillar apostles "added nothing" to his message (2:6) and openly affirmed his ministry by giving him the "right hand of fellowship" (2:9).

2:3 compelled to be circumcised: The Greek expression here and at 6:12 is used by ancient writers like Josephus and Ptolemy to describe forcible circumcision. The idea is historically linked with Jewish military efforts to subjugate neighboring Gentiles during the Maccabean period by forcing them under the yoke of the Mosaic Law (cf. 1 Mac 2:46) and the administration of the Judean State centered in Jerusalem. The Judaizers are doing something analogous in Galatia by insisting that Gentiles submit to circumcision in order to be incorporated into the commonwealth of the covenant people.

2:4 false brethren: Judean believers who promoted circumcision as a necessary prerequisite for salvation (Acts 15:1). **our freedom:** Christ liberates believers from the curses and ceremonies of the Mosaic Law (3:13; 5:6; 6:15). The danger here is that the Judaizers will enslave the Galatians if they successfully persuade them to receive circumcision (5:1–3).

2:6 reputed to be something: The Jerusalem apostles were held in high esteem. Though his tone seems distant and cool, Paul neither affirms nor denies them this honor.

2:7 uncircumcised . . . circumcised: Epithets for Gentiles and Israelites, respectively (Eph 2:11–12). This does not mean the divisions of missionary labor were drawn along purely geographical lines, since Peter traveled extensively and Paul also evangelized his Israelite kinsmen living among the Gentiles. See note on Acts 13:5.

2:9 James and Cephas and John: I.e., James, the brother of the Lord (1:19), Simon Peter (Jn 1:42), and John, the son of Zebedee (Mt 10:2). The order of the names is unusual, as Peter is always mentioned first in the apostolic lists of the NT (Mt 10:2; Mk 3:16; Jn 21:2; Acts 1:13). Perhaps Paul lists James first as a way of undercutting the claims of the Judaizers, who, along with other Jewish conservatives, had a deep respect for James as the spiritual shepherd of the Jerusalem Church at this time (after Peter fled the city, Acts 12:17). By stressing that *James* endorsed his gospel, Paul shows that the Judaizers have no official backing from Jerusalem, even from its most conser-

vative leadership. For more on James, see note on 1:19. **pillars:** Important leaders in the Church, which is pictured as the living Temple of God (Rev 3:12; cf. Eph 2:19–22).

2:10 remember the poor: This was the inspiration behind Paul's effort to collect charitable contributions for the believers in Jerusalem living in poverty (Rom 15:26; 2 Cor 8–9). The Galatians themselves donated to this fund (1 Cor 16:1-3).

2:11 Antioch: The capital of the Roman province of Syria, north of Palestine. The Antiochene Church was the first to bring Christian Jews and Gentiles together in fellowship (Acts 11:19-26) and the first to organize missionary outreaches to the Gentiles (Acts 13:1-3). **Cephas** probably came to the city after the Jerusalem Council, as did Paul and Barnabas (Acts 15:35).

2:12 separated himself: Peter reverts to the custom of traditional Judaism, which discouraged social contact, especially shared meals, between Jews and Gentiles (Acts 10:28; *Jubilees* 22, 16). It was feared, among other things, that Gentile food might violate the purity standards of the Torah, i.e., it might be either unclean or improperly prepared (Lev 11:1-47; 17:10-13). The problem here is that Peter has already been informed that the Jewish dietary laws have been set aside in the New Covenant and that Gentiles are now welcome members of the family of faith (Acts 10:9-16, 28). **men came from James:** Either a delegation sent by James or loyal associates of James who came on their own initiative. The former seems more likely, but for the possibility of the latter, see Acts 15:24. **the circumcision party:** Jewish Christians who discouraged table fellowship between Jews and Gentiles. Peter had been criticized by them on this issue once before (Acts 11:2-3).

■ **2:14 before them all:** It is precisely Peter's authority and influence in the Church that made it necessary for Paul to correct him in public. **to live like Jews:** Literally, "to Judaize", or "to adopt Jewish customs". Peter's conduct implied the very thing he had denied at the Jerusalem Council, namely, that Gentile Christians must adopt the ritual laws of Judaism in order to secure their standing in the covenant and obtain salvation (Acts 15:7-11). ● The same expression is used once in the Greek OT, where it describes how Gentiles from Persia were "circumcised" and "Judaized" for fear of the Jews (Esther 8:17). Here too, in the case of Peter (2:12) as well as the Judaizers (6:12), fear is once again the driving force behind the impulse to Judaize.

■ **2:16 justified:** Established in a right relationship with God. Justification involves the cleansing of sin, the

---

[d] Or *reckoned righteous*; and so elsewhere.

by works of the law but through faith in Jesus Christ, even we have believed in Christ Jesus, in order to be justified by faith in Christ, and not by works of the law, because by works of the law shall no flesh be justified. [17]But if, in our endeavor to be justified in Christ, we ourselves were found to be sinners, is Christ then an agent of sin? Certainly not! [18]But if I build up again those things which I tore down, then I prove myself a transgressor. [19]For I through the law died to the law, that I might live to God. [20]I have been crucified with Christ; it is no longer I who live, but Christ who lives in me; and the life I now live in the flesh I live by faith in the Son of God, who loved me and gave himself for me. [21]I do not nullify the grace of God; for if justification [e] were through the law, then Christ died to no purpose.

Law or Faith

3 O foolish Galatians! Who has bewitched you, before whose eyes Jesus Christ was publicly portrayed as crucified? [2]Let me ask you only this: Did you receive the Spirit by works of the law, or by hearing with faith? [3]Are you so foolish? Having begun with the Spirit, are you now ending with the flesh? [4]Did you experience so many things in vain?—if it really is in vain. [5]Does he who supplies the Spirit to you and works miracles among you do so by works of the law, or by hearing with faith?

6 Thus Abraham "believed God, and it was reckoned to him as righteousness." [7]So you see that it is men of faith who are the sons of Abraham. [8]And the Scripture, foreseeing that God would justify the Gentiles by faith, preached the gospel beforehand to Abraham, saying, "In you shall all the nations be blessed." [9]So then, those who are men of faith are blessed with Abraham who had faith.

10 For all who rely on works of the law are under a curse; for it is written, "Cursed be every one who does not abide by all things written in the

---

2:20: Gal 1:4.   **3:6:** Gen 15:6; Rom 4:3.   **3:8:** Gen 12:3; 18:18; Acts 3:25.   **3:9:** Rom 4:16.
3:10: Deut 27:26.   **3:11:** Hab 2:4; Rom 1:17; Heb 10:38.

---

infusion of divine life, and the adoption of the believer into the family of God through Baptism (1 Cor 6:11; Tit 3:5) (CCC 1987–95). See word study: *Justified* at Rom 2:13. **works of the law:** See essay: *The Works of the Law.* **shall no flesh be justified:** Identical to the statement in Rom 3:20 and probably an allusion to the Greek version of Ps 143:2. • The Psalmist begs the Lord to suspend judgment on his life, for he knows that no one is without fault and thus no one can stand before God in perfect righteousness. • Some claim that if no one is justified by the law, but only by faith in Christ, then the Patriarchs and Prophets who lived before Christ were imperfect. The saints of old, however, were justified by faith in Christ (St. Jerome, *Commentary on Galatians* 2:16).
2:17 found to be sinners: I.e., living like Gentiles, who do not follow the Mosaic Law (2:15).
2:18 which I tore down: The Torah stood as a protective barrier between the idolatry of the Gentiles (Lev 15:31; 20:26). This dividing wall of separation has now been dismantled by Christ (Eph 2:14), who brings Jews and Gentiles together in the New Covenant (3:28).
2:20 crucified with Christ: United with the Cross, Paul has died to an old order of things, namely, the slavery of sin and the regime of the Old Covenant. He describes this elsewhere as a sacramental union with Jesus effected through Baptism (Rom 6:3–8). **lives in me:** Believers possess life that is natural and biological (human life) as well as supernatural and theological (divine life). **who loved me:** Jesus endured the torture and shame of the Cross for the entire world collectively and for every person individually (CCC 478, 616).
2:21 died to no purpose: Paul reasons that if the Mosaic Law had been sufficient all along to remove sin, establish us in righteousness, and bring us into God's family, then the Cross would have been completely unnecessary (3:21). • The Law can neither remit sin nor triumph over eternal death nor free those held captive because of sin. Christ died to provide those things that the Law could not (Ambrosiaster, *Commentary on Galatians* 2:21).
3:1 O foolish Galatians: Paul is irked and dismayed that his readers have succumbed to the pressure of the Judaizers (1:6). **portrayed as crucified:** The Galatians did not witness the Crucifixion of Jesus in person but embraced the message of the Cross that Paul so vividly proclaimed (1 Cor 1:18, 23).

3:2 hearing with faith?: The Galatian controversy turns on the question of *when* they received the Holy Spirit. Since this happened when they believed the gospel and were baptized (Acts 2:38), Paul deems it foolish to accept circumcision and other **works** of the Mosaic Law as additional requirements needed to complete their Christian initiation. This is the very logic set forth by Peter at the Jerusalem Council (Acts 15:8–11).
3:4 experience: This could also be translated "suffer" and may indicate that some, like the Judaizers themselves, were tempted to accept circumcision because of Jewish persecution (6:12).
3:6 Abraham: The great-grandfather of Israel by race and the father of all believers by grace. Paul sees the gospel of justification proclaimed in the life of Abraham, who was righteous by faith completely apart from his circumcision (Rom 4:9–12). **believed God:** A citation from Gen 15:6. • This was a time of testing for Abraham, when God was stretching his faith in a moment of discouragement (1 Mac 2:52). Though faced with formidable obstacles, such as his age and the barrenness of his wife, he trusted that God could do the impossible by giving him a son. The promise was later fulfilled in the birth of Isaac (Gen 21:1–3). It is clear from the context of Genesis, as well as Heb 11:8–12, that this is not the moment of Abraham's conversion, for it is not the first time he puts his faith in the Lord. For details, see note on Gen 15:6.
3:8 all the nations be blessed: The citation combines the Greek version of Gen 12:3 and Gen 18:18. • God promised blessings for Abraham that extended well beyond both his tribal family and his lifetime. It was a promise of worldwide salvation to come (CCC 59–61).
3:10 Cursed be every one: A citation from Deut 27:26. • This is the final and climactic curse that Israel invoked upon itself in the oath ceremony that ratified the Deuteronomic covenant. In the subsequent context, Moses predicted the rebellion and cursing of Israel (Deut 28:47–68) as well as the eventual restoration and blessing of Israel (Deut 30:1–10). It is possible this passage was used by the Judaizers to insist on the necessity of circumcision, lest nonobservance of the Law result in a curse. Paul, however, uses it against them, charging that everyone who embraces the Law embraces the curse, for not even the Judaizers follow all of its demands to perfection (6:13). **book of the law:** A technical term for the Book of Deuteronomy (Deut 29:21; 30:10), which was written on a scroll and placed

---

[e] Or *righteousness*.

The Works of the Law

E IGHT TIMES in his letters Paul uses the expression "works of the law", twice in Romans (Rom 3:20, 28) and six times in Galatians (Gal 2:16; 3:2, 5, 10). Each time he denies these works the power to save us and subjects them to theological critique. Paul is intent on convincing his Roman and Galatian readers that, unlike faith in Jesus Christ, the "works of the law" neither justify the sinner nor confer the Spirit on believers.

But what are the "works of the law"? According to some, Paul uses this expression to refer to legalism, that is, the misguided attempt to amass favor with God and to earn salvation for oneself by the performance of good works. On this reading, Paul is said to reject all attempts to merit eternal life by sheer human effort. According to others, Paul is talking about obedience to the Mosaic Law as a path that leads to salvation. On this reading, Paul is said to stress the problem of human weakness and man's inability to keep the Law either consistently or comprehensively. Logically, from this perspective, observance of the Law cannot justify the sinner before God because no one can obey the Law without fault.

THE PRIMARY MEANING

These views are true at the theological level, and other passages of Scripture indicate that Paul made important assertions to this effect, but several modern scholars believe Paul had something more specific in mind when he used the "works of the law" formula. According to these scholars, Paul used this phrase to refer primarily to the *Mosaic ceremonial works*. It is mainly the visible expressions of Jewish life and identity, like circumcision, dietary regulations, purity codes, Sabbath observance, and the liturgical calendar of Old Covenant feasts, that Paul contrasts with faith. These are the ritual distinctives that set Jews apart from Gentiles in the Hellenistic world of the first century. In support of this thesis, its advocates note how this issue consistently surfaces when Paul is talking about the salvation of Jews and Gentiles. They likewise point out, from the wider context of Romans and Galatians, that the apostle stresses the irrelevance of ceremonial rites like circumcision (Rom 2:25-29; 3:30; 4:9-12; Gal 2:3; 5:2-12; 6:12-15), dietary issues (Rom 14:1-23; Gal 2:11-14), and feast-day observances (Rom 14:5-6; Gal 4:10). Though the point is contested, some see corroborating evidence for this view in the Dead Sea Scrolls, where the Hebrew equivalent of "works of the law" (*ma'ase hattorah*) turns up in a context where laws concerning purity, sacrifice, festivals, and foods are the central issues of discussion (scroll fragment 4QMMT).

Interestingly enough, this new perspective on "works of the law" is actually a very old one. The Alexandrian scholar Origen put forth the substance of this interpretation as early as the third century (*Commentary on Romans* 8, 7, 6). Saint Jerome connected the phrase with the ceremonial rituals in the fourth century (*Commentary on Galatians* at Gal 2:19), as did his contemporary Ambrosiaster in his Latin commentary on the Pauline epistles (*Commentary on Romans* at Rom 3:28). The same interpretation was made in the fifth century by the Greek scholar and bishop Theodoret of Cyrrhus (*Commentary on Galatians* at Gal 2:15-16). In medieval times, Saint Thomas Aquinas favored this as the primary meaning, asserting that the theme of Galatians "concerns the termination of the Old Testament sacraments" (*Commentary on Galatians* 1, 1). Select comments from the founders of Protestantism indicate that Catholic theologians were linking the works of the Law with its ceremonies in the sixteenth century as well (see, e.g., John Calvin, *Commentary on Galatians* at Gal 2:15; Martin Chemnitz, *Examination of the Council of Trent, Concerning Justification* 3, 5).

Thus, in the history of Catholic scholarship, there has consistently been an identification of the "works" of the Mosaic Law with its ritual "ceremonies". That is not to say that this amounts to a consensus position, as many have taken a broader line of interpretation (e.g., St. Augustine, *On the Spirit and the Letter* 23). But acceptance of the ceremonial reading remains attractive because it makes excellent sense of Paul's polemical engagement with Jews and Gentiles on the question of salvation and the means of justification. Beyond this, it invites deeper theological reflection on the purpose of these rites in the economy of salvation.

THE THEOLOGICAL MEANING

The theology that underlies the Mosaic ceremonies is rich and manifold. To understand it is to understand better why Paul pits the works of the Law over against faith in Christ. **(1)** The ceremonial laws expressed a theology of separation that is proper to the Old Covenant. For centuries, works such as circumcision, food restrictions, observance of the Sabbath, etc., functioned as badges of Israel's election that made the Jews a people distinct from the Gentiles. But when Christ came to gather all nations into the fold of the New Covenant, the ceremonial boundaries that divided Israel from the rest of world were set aside as outdated and expired. Because the Church is an international community that includes Jews but does not exclude Gentiles, the rituals exclusive to Judaism are no longer appropriate for marking out the People of God (Rom 1:5, 16; 3:29-30; Gal 3:28). **(2)** The Mosaic rituals were mere shadows of

Continued

book of the law, and do them." [11]Now it is evident that no man is justified before God by the law; for "He who through faith is righteous shall live"; [f] [12]but the law does not rest on faith, for "He who does them shall live by them." [13]Christ redeemed us from the curse of the law, having become a curse for us—for it is written, "Cursed be every one who hangs on a tree"—[14]that in Christ Jesus the bless-ing of Abraham might come upon the Gentiles, that we might receive the promise of the Spirit through faith.

The Promise to Abraham

15 To give a human example, brethren: no one annuls even a man's will, [g] or adds to it, once it has been ratified. [16]Now the promises were made to Abraham and to his offspring. It does not say, "And

---

3:12: Lev 18:5; Rom 10:5.   **3:13:** Deut 21:23.   **3:16:** Gen 12:7.   **3:17:** Ex 12:40.

---

beside the Ark of the Covenant (Deut 31:26). Some read it with reference to the Mosaic Law more generally.

3:11 He who through faith: A citation from Hab 2:4.
● Habakkuk is assured that, despite the coming invasion of Judea by the Babylonians, the one who clings to the Lord in faith will be given the grace of protection and will survive the catastrophe. From this text Paul hails faith, not observance of the Law, as the foundation of justification (3:21–22; Rom 1:17).

3:12 He who does them: A citation from Lev 18:5.
● Leviticus promises life to Israel for observing the Torah and shunning the sins of the Gentiles. Yet, as the recurring transgressions of Israel show (Neh 9:29), the Mosaic Law did not come with the grace needed to keep it (Rom 8:4). Paul may be interpreting this passage through the lens of Ezek 20:11, 13, 21, where the Prophet contrasts the Levitical promise of life given at Sinai with the Deuteronomic promises of curse and death issued on the plains of Moab (Ezek 20:25–26).

3:13 Cursed be every one: A citation from Deut 21:23.
● This refers to the practice of hanging executed criminals on trees to avert the wrath of God (Num 25:4; 2 Sam 21:9). For Paul, Jesus bore the curses pressing down upon Israel when he mounted the Cross (Gal 3:10). This act enabled the blessings of the Abrahamic covenant, held back for centu-

ries because of the curse, to pour forth upon Israel and the world as a result (3:14; CCC 580). The Dead Sea Scrolls like-wise associate crucifixion with the curse of Deut 21:22–23.

3:14 the blessing of Abraham: I.e., the Spirit, which is the messianic blessing revealed by the Prophets (Is 44:3; Ezek 36:26–27; Joel 2:28). ● The exact expression is from Gen 28:4, where Isaac confers the blessing of Abraham upon his son Jacob. This shows that Isaac alone was the bearer of the Abrahamic blessing, not Ishmael or any other of Abraham's sons (Rom 9:7–9). Paul will capitalize on the significance of this in 3:16 and 4:28.

3:15–18 The major premise of Paul's covenant theology in Galatians, namely, that Israel's failure to keep the *Mosaic* covenant did not relieve God of his prior obligation to fulfill the *Abrahamic* covenant ratified centuries earlier. Since even human covenants are inviolable once they are ratified by oath, the covenant oath that God swore to Abraham is even more so (Gen 22:16–18; Heb 6:13–18). Not even the ratification of subsequent covenants under Moses could alter or annul God's unconditional pledge to bless the world through Abraham's offspring. In effect, then, the Abrahamic covenant both precedes and supercedes the Mosaic covenant that came after it.

3:15 will: The term means "testament" or "will" in secular Greek usage but "covenant" in biblical Greek usage. Despite

---

[f] Or *the righteous shall live by faith.*
[g] Or *covenant* (as in verse 17).

---

better things to come in Christ (Col 2:16–17). In other words, the ceremonies of the Law were signs of grace but not sacraments of grace; they pointed the way to the benefits we receive in Christ, but they did not confer those benefits (Heb 7:18–19; 10:1–4). So, for example, circumcision of the flesh prefigured the inward grace that transforms the heart in Baptism (Col 2:11–12). The sacrifices of the Mosaic Law set the stage for the perfect sacrifice of Jesus, which alone effects a true remission of sins (Heb 10:11–18). Festivals such as Passover likewise prepared Israel to receive the true Lamb of God as holy food (1 Cor 5:7–8; 10:16). All the ceremonies, in one way or another, served a prophetic function that was important in the old economy but was no longer necessary once Christ came and fulfilled what had long ago been foreshadowed. **(3)** The Mosaic ceremonies were symbolic rituals that taught important lessons about divine grace and the inadequacy of human works. In concert with the Mosaic Law as a whole, the ceremonial laws were part of a divine education in humility and the need for grace. Take circumcision, for example. At one level, it is a sign of the righteousness Abraham possessed by faith (Rom 4:11). At another, it is a reminder that God fulfills his plan by grace rather than human works. Recall that circumcision was given (Gen 17:1–17) after Abraham had grown impatient and tried to accomplish by his own efforts (Gen 16:1–6) what only God could do for him by a miracle of grace, namely, give him a son in old age (Gen 15:4). Circumcision, it would seem, was a painful reminder to Abraham of this important lesson. Likewise, Sabbath observance was a weekly reminder that man's work, accomplished in six days, must desist and give way to a celebration of God's works on the seventh day (creation, Ex 20:11; redemption, Deut 5:15). Sacrifice had a pedagogical purpose as well, serving as an ongoing memorial of human weakness and sin (Heb 10:3). On the one hand, God instituted sacrifice to express his desire to be forgiving to his wayward people. On the other, by ordering the continuous cycle of offerings under the Old Covenant, he was driving home the point that man is weak and powerless to avoid transgressions by his own strength and so stands in need of grace and divine mercy.

All of this helps us to bring Paul's teaching into focus. Far from justifying the sinner, the ceremonial "works" declare that man is weak and sinful and in desperate need of God's help. In effect, they show us our needs without meeting our needs. Instead of providing a solution to our problem, they point beyond themselves to the ultimate solution provided by God in the dying and rising of Jesus Christ for our salvation. «

to offsprings," referring to many; but, referring to one, "And to your offspring," which is Christ. [17]This is what I mean: the law, which came four hundred and thirty years afterward, does not annul a covenant previously ratified by God, so as to make the promise void. [18]For if the inheritance is by the law, it is no longer by promise; but God gave it to Abraham by a promise.

The Purpose of the Law

[19] Why then the law? It was added because of transgressions, till the offspring should come to whom the promise had been made; and it was ordained by angels through an intermediary. [20]Now an intermediary implies more than one; but God is one.

[21] Is the law then against the promises of God? Certainly not; for if a law had been given which could make alive, then righteousness would indeed be by the law. [22]But the Scripture consigned all things to sin, that what was promised to faith in Jesus Christ might be given to those who believe.

[23] Now before faith came, we were confined under the law, kept under restraint until faith should be revealed. [24]So that the law was our custodian until Christ came, that we might be justified by faith. [25]But now that faith has come, we are no longer under a custodian; [26]for in Christ Jesus you are all sons of God, through faith. [27]For as many of you as were baptized into Christ have put on Christ. [28]There is neither Jew nor Greek, there is neither slave nor free, there is neither male nor female; for you are all one in Christ Jesus. [29]And if you are Christ's, then you are Abraham's offspring, heirs according to promise.

3:18: Rom 11:6.   **3:19:** Rom 5:20.   **3:21:** Rom 8:2–4.   **3:22:** Rom 3:9–19; 11:32.   **3:28:** Rom 10:12.

---

the RSV translation, the biblical sense of "covenant" is probably intended here, since (1) Paul uses the term this way in his other writings (Rom 9:4; 11:27; 2 Cor 3:6, 14; Eph 2:12), (2) he uses it this way elsewhere in Galatians (3:17; 4:24), and (3) it is a known fact that a will in Greco-Roman antiquity could be altered or even annulled after the death of the testator who drafted it, which is the very point Paul denies in this verse. For a similar translation issue in Hebrews, see essay: *Will or Covenant?* at Heb 9.

3:16 And to his offspring: A reference to Gen 22:18. ● Paul is alluding to the covenant oath that God swore to Abraham to bless all nations through Isaac and his descendants (Sir 44:21; CCC 706). It is significant for Paul that Abraham's other son, Ishmael, was disinherited in the preceding chapter and thus excluded from this covenant (Gen 21:10–12). Thus, when Paul stresses that the word "offspring" is singular rather than plural, he is (1) alluding to the divine election of Isaac over Ishmael in the Genesis narrative (Gal 4:28–31; Rom 9:7–8) and (2) implying that Isaac is a type of Christ, so that the act that elicits the promised blessing (the sacrifice of Isaac) prefigures the act that fulfills it (the sacrifice of Jesus). See note on Rom 8:32.

3:17 four hundred and thirty years: The duration of Israel's stay in Egypt before the Exodus (Ex 12:40–41). Thus, the Abrahamic covenant, last confirmed with Jacob (Gen 28:14), preceded the ratification of the Mosaic covenant by more than four centuries (Ex 19–24).

3:19 It was added: The Torah was inserted into history between the Abrahamic covenant and the New Covenant. **because of:** The Greek can indicate either the goal ("for the sake of") or the cause ("by reason of") for adding the Law. Paul may have both ideas in mind: the *goal* of the Law was to expose transgressions and heighten Israel's awareness of sin (Rom 3:20; 5:20; 7:7); the *cause* for adding the Law, at least the bulk of its sacrificial and ceremonial rites, was the rebellion of Israel during the Exodus period, particularly the golden calf transgression (see, e.g., Christian theologians St. Justin Martyr, *Dialogue with Trypho* 18–22; St. Irenaeus, *Against Heresies* 4, 15; St. Aphrahat, *Demonstrations* 15, 8; St. Thomas Aquinas, *Summa Theologiae* I-II, 102, 3). **ordained by angels:** Jewish tradition based on the Greek version of Deut 33:2 held that Moses received the Torah from the hands of the angels (Acts 7:53; Heb 2:2; Josephus, *Antiquities* 15, 136).

3:20 an intermediary: Moses, who delivered the Torah to Israel (Ex 20:18–22; Deut 5:4–5). That the Mosaic covenant involved a mediator implied that **more than one** party was responsible for fulfilling the terms of the covenant—God and Israel. The Abrahamic covenant, by contrast, was a unilateral arrangement, i.e., God alone swore an oath and assumed the

responsibility of blessing the world through Abraham's offspring (Gen 22:16–18). **God is one:** The monotheistic creed of ancient Israel (Deut 6:4).

3:22 consigned all things to sin: Scripture declares all peoples, Jews and Gentiles alike, prisoners of sin. Paul spells this out in Rom 3:9–19 and Rom 11:32.

3:23 kept under restraint: The mass of ethical, juridical, and ceremonial laws codified in the Torah was designed to keep Israel in temporary protective custody, lest it imitate the depravity of the Gentiles (CCC 1963–64).

3:27 baptized into Christ: Baptism is the sacrament of faith (3:26) and the rite of Christian initiation that replaces circumcision (Col 2:11–12). It cleanses us of sin, joins us with Christ, and makes us righteous children of God (Acts 22:16; Tit 3:5; 1 Pet 3:21; CCC 1226–27). Paul's description of this mystery reflects early liturgical practice where the newly baptized **put on** a white garment to symbolize their purity in **Christ** (cf. Rom 13:14; Eph 4:24; CCC 1243, 2348).

3:28 you are all one: All peoples, irrespective of ethnic, gender, and social distinctions, are equal candidates for salvation and sonship in Christ (Col 3:11; CCC 791).

Word Study

Custodian (Gal 3:24–25)

Paidagōgos (Gk.): a "tutor" or "disciplinarian" or "guide". The word is used twice in the NT, here and at 1 Cor 4:15. It refers to a household slave in Hellenistic society who was charged by a father to oversee the moral formation of his son. This tutelage normally lasted from the time the child was a minor until he reached maturity. The tutor would accompany the youth to and from school, supervise his daily activities, protect him from dangers, and administer discipline whenever necessary. Paul used this familiar custom to explain how the Mosaic Law served a similar function in Israel. It was an instructor and guide for the nation, yet one that was temporary and destined to pass away. The coming of Christ meant that Israel could now be freed from the supervision and restraints of the Mosaic Law to embrace the full inheritance awaiting it in the New Covenant (Gal 4:4–7; CCC 708).

4 I mean that the heir, as long as he is a child, is no better than a slave, though he is the owner of all the estate; ²but he is under guardians and trustees until the date set by the father. ³So with us; when we were children, we were slaves to the elemental spirits of the universe. ⁴But when the time had fully come, God sent forth his Son, born of woman, born under the law, ⁵to redeem those who were under the law, so that we might receive adoption as sons. ⁶And because you are sons, God has sent the Spirit of his Son into our hearts, crying, "Abba! Father!" ⁷So through God you are no longer a slave but a son, and if a son then an heir.

Paul Reproves the Galatians

8 Formerly, when you did not know God, you were in bondage to beings that by nature are no gods; ⁹but now that you have come to know God, or rather to be known by God, how can you turn back again to the weak and beggarly elemental spirits, whose slaves you want to be once more? ¹⁰You observe days, and months, and seasons, and years! ¹¹I am afraid I have labored over you in vain.

12 Brethren, I beg you, become as I am, for I also have become as you are. You did me no wrong; ¹³you know it was because of a bodily ailment that I preached the gospel to you at first; ¹⁴and though my condition was a trial to you, you did not scorn

---

4:3: Col 2:20.   **4:6:** Rom 8:15.

4:1–7 Paul reads the history of Israel as the story of a minor who has grown to maturity and is ready to receive his inheritance. During the Exodus, Israel was a rebellious son (Ex 4:22) whom Yahweh placed under the guardianship of the Mosaic Law (3:24) and the servile discipline of covenant curses (3:13). The coming of Christ marks the appointed time when the curses and ceremonies of the Mosaic Law are finally set aside and Israel can receive the full inheritance of sonship through the Spirit (Rom 8:14–15; CCC 1972).

4:3 elemental spirits: The Greek word is simply "elements", which can denote (1) the first principles of education (Heb 5:12), (2) the physical elements of the world (2 Pet 3:10), (3) the heavenly bodies and luminaries, which were deified by the pagans (cf. Deut 4:19), or (4) the spirits that control the cosmic elements and were likewise worshiped by the pagans (cf. Wis 13:2). Each of these has connections with the religious culture of the Hellenistic world. In this context, however, life under the elements is connected with life under the Law (3:23–25). The point is not that Judaism is no different from paganism, but that both constitute a state of bondage under cosmic forces from which Christ has freed us (4:4–5, 8–9; Col 2:8, 20). Perhaps the Torah is classified with the elements because it teaches rudimentary principles of religion; its legal observances make use of physical substances; its cultic calendar follows the movements of the sun and moon; and the Law is mediated by angelic spirits (3:19), who, according to Jewish tradition, stand in charge of the physical elements and seasonal cycles of the world (*Jubilees* 2, 2).

4:4 the time had fully come: History reached a climax with the birth and death of the Messiah (Mk 1:15; Eph 1:10). This was the predetermined date "set" by God the Father to confer the blessing of divine sonship upon both Israel and the Gentiles (4:2; CCC 422, 484). **born of woman:** Emphasizes that Jesus shared in the human condition (Job 14:1; Mt 11:11). Giving birth and flesh to the Son of God makes Mary the Mother of God (CCC 495, 723). See note on Lk 1:43. **born under the law:** Emphasizes Jesus' link with Judaism and his messianic mission to rescue Israel from the slavery of the Law and its covenant curses (3:13; CCC 580).

4:6 sent the Spirit: As the Father sent the Son to redeem all nations from sin (4:4), he likewise sent the Spirit to renew them for a life of sanctity. The joint mission of the Son and Spirit is to bring blessing to the whole human family and unify them in the divine family of God (CCC 689). **into our hearts:** The Spirit fills us with God's presence and love (Rom 5:5; 2 Cor 1:22). His divine assistance enables us to live righteously as sons and daughters of the Father (Rom 8:4; 1 Jn 3:7; CCC 1265–66, 1695). **Abba!:** Aramaic for "Father!" It bespeaks a new level of intimacy with the Father that Jesus opened (Mk 14:36) for the children of God (Rom 8:15) (CCC 683, 2766).

4:8–11 Paul's personal appeal to the Galatians. Having refuted the logic of the Judaizers in 3:1–4:7, he now urges readers to repudiate their propaganda. The pastoral tone of this section reveals the depth of Paul's affection for the Galatians and indicates how earnestly he wants to restore them to spiritual health.

4:8 you did not know God: The Galatians were once pagans, ignorant of the God of Israel (Ps 79:6; 1 Thess 4:5). In accepting the gospel, they turned away from lifeless idols to be known and loved by the living God (4:9; 1 Thess 1:9).

4:9 elemental spirits: For the meaning of this, see note on 4:3.

4:10 days . . . months . . . seasons . . . years: Refers to the liturgical calendar of Israel, which was regulated by the cycles of the sun and moon (Gen 1:14). Apparently the Judaizers persuaded some of the Galatians to begin celebrating the weekly (Sabbath, Ex 20:8–11), monthly (New Moon, Num 28:11–15), seasonal (Passover, Pentecost, etc., Deut 16:1–17), and yearly (New Years, see note on Lev 23:24) festivals of the Old Covenant (Col 2:16).

4:12 become as I am: Imitating Paul in this context means putting aside the ritual ordinances of the Mosaic Law to "live like a Gentile and not like a Jew" (2:14).

4:13 a bodily ailment: The infirmity is not specified, but Paul's comments in 4:15 and 6:11 suggest it may have been a visual handicap.

Word Study

Adoption (Gal 4:5)

Huiothesia (Gk.): means "adoption as sons" and can refer to the process of entering a new family or to its lasting result. Paul uses the term five times in the NT. In Rom 9:4, he lists it among the privileges that Israel enjoyed by virtue of its covenant bond with Yahweh (Ex 4:22; Hos 1:11). Every other use of the word is connected with Christians. For Paul, the divine adoption of the believer takes place in two stages: first, our souls are raised to new life and filled with the grace of divine sonship (Rom 8:15; Eph 1:5) and, finally, our bodies will be raised to new life and filled with the glory of divine sonship (Rom 8:23). Divine adoption results from an infusion of the divine life of the Spirit (Gal 4:5–6). Historically, the gift of sonship once possessed in part by Israel is now granted in full to all nations united with Christ through faith and Baptism (Gal 3:26–27). While Christ alone is the natural Son of God, we are made to share in his filial life as adopted "sons in the Son".

or despise me, but received me as an angel of God, as Christ Jesus. ¹⁵What has become of the satisfaction you felt? For I bear you witness that, if possible, you would have plucked out your eyes and given them to me. ¹⁶Have I then become your enemy by telling you the truth?ʰ ¹⁷They make much of you, but for no good purpose; they want to shut you out, that you may make much of them. ¹⁸For a good purpose it is always good to be made much of, and not only when I am present with you. ¹⁹My little children, with whom I am again in travail until Christ be formed in you! ²⁰I could wish to be present with you now and to change my tone, for I am perplexed about you.

The Allegory of Hagar and Sarah

21 Tell me, you who desire to be under law, do you not hear the law? ²²For it is written that Abraham had two sons, one by a slave and one by a free woman. ²³But the son of the slave was born according to the flesh, the son of the free woman through promise. ²⁴Now this is an allegory: these women are two covenants. One is from Mount Sinai, bearing children for slavery; she is Hagar. ²⁵Now

Hagar is Mount Sinai in Arabia;ⁱ she corresponds to the present Jerusalem, for she is in slavery with her children. ²⁶But the Jerusalem above is free, and she is our mother. ²⁷For it is written,

"Rejoice, O barren one who does not bear;
break forth and shout, you who are not with
        labor pains;
for the desolate has more children
than she who has a husband."

²⁸Now we,ʲ brethren, like Isaac, are children of promise. ²⁹But as at that time he who was born according to the flesh persecuted him who was born according to the Spirit, so it is now. ³⁰But what does the Scripture say? "Cast out the slave and her son; for the son of the slave shall not inherit with the son of the free woman." ³¹So, brethren, we are not children of the slave but of the free woman.

Christian Freedom

5 For freedom Christ has set us free; stand fast therefore, and do not submit again to a yoke of slavery.

2 Now I, Paul, say to you that if you receive

4:13: Acts 16:6.   **4:19:** 1 Cor 4:15.   **4:22:** Gen 16:15; 21:2, 9.   **4:23:** Rom 9:7–9.
4:27: Is 54:1.   **4:29:** Gen 21:9.   **4:30:** Gen 21:10–12.

4:19 in travail: Paul describes himself as a mother who begot Christ in the lives of the Galatians (cf. 2:20). His labor pains continue as he groans to see his sons and daughters turning back to bondage (CCC 526, 562).

4:22 two sons: Abraham's oldest son, Ishmael, was born of his concubine, Hagar (Gen 16:15), while his younger son, Isaac, was born of his wife, Sarah (Gen 21:1–3). Hagar was Sarah's personal slave (Gen 16:1).

4:23 through promise: The birth of Isaac was the result of God's promise and miraculous intervention, since Sarah was barren and elderly at the time (Gen 15:2–4; 17:15–19). Ishmael was conceived by purely natural means, that is, according to the flesh (Gen 16:3–4).

4:24–31 The mothers of Isaac and Ishmael represent two distinct covenants and thus two ages of salvation history. The slave woman, **Hagar**, is linked with **Mount Sinai**, where the Torah was given to Israel; the essence of this covenant was practiced and promoted in **Jerusalem**. The free woman, Sarah, is symbolic of the heavenly **Jerusalem above**, where the saints worship God in the freedom of the New Covenant (Heb 12:22–23) without the burdensome yoke of the Mosaic Law (5:1). A contrast is thus set up between the Judaizers and the Galatians: the former are sons of the earthly Jerusalem, who are born into religious slavery through the Law (like Ishmael, from Hagar), while the latter are sons of the heavenly Jerusalem (CCC 757), who are born into freedom and blessedness through the gospel (like Isaac, from Sarah). See note on 3:15–18.

4:24 this is an allegory: An example of spiritual exegesis, which expounds the prophetic meaning of OT persons, places, events, and institutions in light of the New Covenant. Whereas literal exegesis interprets the words of the Bible, spiritual exegesis interprets the realities and events of the Bible described by its words (CCC 115–17). ● The author of Holy Scripture is God, who can signify his meaning, not only by words, as even man can do, but also by things. The first signification whereby words signify things belongs to the historical or literal sense. The signification whereby things signified by words

also have their own signification is the spiritual sense, which is based on the literal and presupposes it (St. Thomas Aquinas, *Summa Theologiae* I, 1, 10).

4:25 in Arabia: Paul naturally links Hagar with Arabia, since the descendants of her son, Ishmael (Arabs), dwelt in this desert region.

4:27 Rejoice, O barren one: A citation from the Greek version of Is 54:1. ● Isaiah compares Jerusalem, destroyed and desolate after the Exile (586 B.C.), to a barren woman made fruitful by God and to a tent that will spread out to make the nations her children (Is 54:2–3). Historically, the text is an allusion to the matriarch Sarah, who was barren but miraculously gave birth to Isaac. Prophetically, it points to the heavenly Jerusalem, which is the mother city made fruitful by God to bear children from all nations through the gospel.

4:28 children of promise: Paul concludes that those in Christ (3:27) share the Abrahamic blessings that were promised to come through Isaac to the world (3:14). See note on 3:16.

4:29 persecuted: Paul follows a Jewish tradition that interprets the "playing" of Abraham's sons in Gen 21:9 as a power struggle between the boys, with the older Ishmael taunting the younger Isaac. The current harassment by the Judaizers links them with Hagar and the Ishmaelites, whose descendants were among the traditional enemies of the covenant people (1 Chron 5:10; Ps 83:5–6).

4:30 Cast out the slave: A citation from Gen 21:10. ● This is the moment when Ishmael is expelled from Abraham's family and disqualified from being a rightful heir. It refutes the logic of the Judaizers that circumcision is the sign that entitles one to a share in the blessings of Abraham. In effect, Paul is reminding them that Ishmael and Isaac were *both* circumcised, yet Ishmael was disinherited and Isaac alone received his father's blessing. See note on Jn 8:35.

5:1 yoke of slavery: An image of the Mosaic Law, with its burdensome ceremonial requirements (Acts 15:10). It stands in stark contrast to the **freedom** of faith in Jesus Christ (Mt 11:29–30), who alone liberates us from sin and death (Acts 13:38–39; CCC 1972). For Paul, the two are mutually exclusive, since to *accept* the yoke of the Law as a requirement for salvation is to *reject* Christ as the sole foundation of our redemption and spiritual life (2:21). ● The Council of Florence

---

ʰ Or *by dealing truly with you.*
ⁱ Other ancient authorities read *For Sinai is a mountain in Arabia.*
ʲ Other ancient authorities read *you.*

circumcision, Christ will be of no advantage to you. [3]I testify again to every man who receives circumcision that he is bound to keep the whole law. [4]You are severed from Christ, you who would be justified by the law; you have fallen away from grace. [5]For through the Spirit, by faith, we wait for the hope of righteousness. [6]For in Christ Jesus neither circumcision nor uncircumcision is of any avail, but faith working through love. [7]You were running well; who hindered you from obeying the truth? [8]This persuasion is not from him who called you. [9]A little leaven leavens all the dough. [10]I have confidence in the Lord that you will take no other view than mine; and he who is troubling you will bear his judgment, whoever he is. [11]But if I, brethren, still preach circumcision, why am I still persecuted? In that case the stumbling block of the cross has been removed. [12]I wish those who unsettle you would mutilate themselves!

[13] For you were called to freedom, brethren; only do not use your freedom as an opportunity for the flesh, but through love be servants of one another. [14]For the whole law is fulfilled in one word, "You shall love your neighbor as yourself." [15]But if you bite and devour one another take heed that you are not consumed by one another.

The Works of the Flesh
and the Fruit of the Spirit

16 But I say, walk by the Spirit, and do not gratify the desires of the flesh. [17]For the desires of the flesh are against the Spirit, and the desires of the Spirit are against the flesh; for these are opposed to each other, to prevent you from doing what you would. [18]But if you are led by the Spirit you are not under the law. [19]Now the works of the flesh are plain: immorality, impurity, licentiousness, [20]idolatry, sorcery, enmity, strife, jealousy, anger, selfishness, dissension, party spirit, [21]envy, [k] drunkenness, carousing, and the like. I warn you, as I warned you before, that those who do such things shall not inherit the kingdom of God. [22]But the fruit of the Spirit is love, joy, peace, patience, kindness, goodness, faithfulness, [23]gentleness, self-control; against such there is no law. [24]And those who belong to

---

5:6: 1 Cor 7:19; Gal 6:15.   **5:9:** 1 Cor 5:6.   **5:14:** Lev 19:18; Rom 13:8–10.   **5:17:** Rom 7:15–23.   **5:19:** Rom 1:28.

(1442) declared that Christians cannot observe the Mosaic ceremonies of the Old Covenant as necessary for salvation without sinning gravely (*Session* 11). Although it was permitted for Jewish converts to maintain their ancestral traditions in the earliest days of the Church, this grace period ended with the wide dissemination of the gospel. Thereafter neither Jews nor Gentiles could lawfully uphold circumcision, animal sacrifices, or dietary distinctions as legitimate practices in the New Covenant.

5:3 keep the whole law: Circumcision is the doorway into the Old Covenant, and so those who embrace it are obligated to observe the Mosaic Law in its entirety. Ironically, the Judaizers are hypocrites in this regard (6:13).

5:6 faith working through love: Faith alone is insufficient to justify the sinner. If it stands by itself and fails to join with love in acts of generosity and service, it is empty and vain (1 Cor 13:2; Jas 2:14–26). The parallel passage in 1 Cor 7:19, which likewise asserts the irrelevance of circumcision, suggests that Paul associates the labor of faith and love with keeping the moral commandments of God. Love has precisely this focus in Pauline theology (5:13–14; Rom 13:8–10) (CCC 162, 1814).

5:9 A little leaven: Symbolic of a hidden but evil influence (Mt 16:12; 1 Cor 5:6–8). If even a few of Paul's readers submit to circumcision at the insistence of the Judaizers, it could have a disastrous effect upon all the Galatian Christians.

5:11 stumbling block of the cross: In the eyes of the Judaizers, this would consist in the exemption of converts from the ritual demands of the Mosaic Law.

5:12 mutilate themselves: Paul wishes sarcastically that the Judaizers, in their zeal to promote circumcision, would go even farther by castrating themselves (Phil 3:2).

5:13 called to freedom: Christian liberty is not a license to indulge in sin and selfishness. We are free, rather, to mature in grace and become the saints we are called to be (Jn 8:31–32). Once Christ has freed us from sin (Rom 6:20–22), the ceremonies of the Old Law (Acts 15:1–11), the curses of the Law (3:13); and the tyranny of our fallen nature (Rom 8:2), it is grossly irresponsible to despise his grace by reverting to the old ways. This would lead again to spiritual slavery, putting offenders in a worse position than ever before (2 Pet 2:19–22) (CCC 1740–42).

5:14 the whole law: The chief aim of the Torah is to promote the love of God, neighbor, and self (Mt 22:34–40; Rom 13:8–10). Jesus lived this intention of the Law to perfection, so that the law of love has become the "law of Christ" (6:2; 1 Cor 9:21). Our ability to fulfill this law is made possible by the grace of the Spirit (Rom 5:5; 8:4). **You shall love your neighbor:** A citation from Lev 19:18. Observance of this law was sorely needed in Galatia, where the Judaizing crisis spawned bitterness and strife between fellow Christians (5:15).
● It may be asked why the apostle mentions love of neighbor but not love of God. Yet who can love his neighbor if he does not love God, since it is only by the gift of God that one can love his neighbor? Since neither precept can be observed unless the other is observed, it suffices to mention one of them (St. Augustine, *Exposition of Galatians* 45).

5:16–24 Paul alerts readers that a hidden war is waged in the heart of every Christian. It is a struggle between the **Spirit** and our **flesh**, i.e., our fallen nature that inclines us toward evil (Rom 8:5–8). Unless we follow the Spirit's lead, the lusts of the flesh (concupiscence) will dominate our lives and enslave us in sin. When we respond to grace, we enable the Spirit to work powerfully in us by clearing out the vices that lead us away from God. Because of our weaknesses, victory in this struggle is possible but not easy (1 Cor 9:25–27) (CCC 2515–16; 1426; 2744).

5:19 works of the flesh: The sins of the flesh include more than just sins of the body (5:19–21). They consist of every act of immorality and injustice that stems from a disordered love of the world (Jas 4:1–5; 1 Jn 2:15–17). These grave sins sever offenders from Christ (5:4) and will block their entrance into heaven if repentance is neglected (CCC 1470, 1855).

5:21 shall not inherit the kingdom: Even Christians can forfeit their salvation if they stifle the Spirit and submit to the flesh (Rom 6:15–16). Paul posts this warning in several of his letters (Rom 8:12–13; 1 Cor 6:9–10; Eph 5:5).

5:22 the fruit of the Spirit: The indwelling of the Spirit produces holiness in the lives of believers (Mt 12:33; Jn 15:1-6). The first fruit of this divine presence is love, the source of all that is good and the virtue upon which others are built (Rom 5:5; 2 Cor 1:22). It may be significant that Paul says "fruit" (singular) instead of "fruits" (plural), suggesting that life in the Spirit is integrated and whole, not fragmented or divided (CCC 736, 1695, 1832).

5:24 crucified the flesh: Baptism unites believers with the

---

[k] Other ancient authorities add *murder*.

Christ Jesus have crucified the flesh with its passions and desires.

25 If we live by the Spirit, let us also walk by the Spirit. ²⁶Let us have no self-conceit, no provoking of one another, no envy of one another.

Bear One Another's Burdens

6 Brethren, if a man is overtaken in any trespass, you who are spiritual should restore him in a spirit of gentleness. Look to yourself, lest you too be tempted. ²Bear one another's burdens, and so fulfil the law of Christ. ³For if any one thinks he is something, when he is nothing, he deceives himself. ⁴But let each one test his own work, and then his reason to boast will be in himself alone and not in his neighbor. ⁵For each man will have to bear his own load.

6 Let him who is taught the word share all good things with him who teaches.

7 Do not be deceived; God is not mocked, for whatever a man sows, that he will also reap. ⁸For he who sows to his own flesh will from the flesh reap corruption; but he who sows to the Spirit will from the Spirit reap eternal life. ⁹And let us not grow weary in well-doing, for in due season we

shall reap, if we do not lose heart. ¹⁰So then, as we have opportunity, let us do good to all men, and especially to those who are of the household of faith.

Final Admonitions and Benediction

11 See with what large letters I am writing to you with my own hand. ¹²It is those who want to make a good showing in the flesh that would compel you to be circumcised, and only in order that they may not be persecuted for the cross of Christ. ¹³For even those who receive circumcision do not themselves keep the law, but they desire to have you circumcised that they may glory in your flesh. ¹⁴But far be it from me to glory except in the cross of our Lord Jesus Christ, by which [1] the world has been crucified to me, and I to the world. ¹⁵For neither circumcision counts for anything, nor uncircumcision, but a new creation. ¹⁶Peace and mercy be upon all who walk by this rule, upon the Israel of God.

17 Henceforth let no man trouble me; for I bear on my body the marks of Jesus.

18 The grace of our Lord Jesus Christ be with your spirit, brethren. Amen.

6:11: 1 Cor 16:21. **6:16:** Ps 125:5.

---

saving death of Jesus, so much so that Paul says we are "crucified with Christ" (2:20; Rom 6:3–4). In addition to receiving forgiveness, we die to our former way of life through the Spirit, who gives us new strength to master our **passions** and selfish **desires** (Rom 7:21–8:2) (CCC 2543, 2848).

6:1 restore him: Fraternal correction is an unpleasant but necessary task to promote the welfare of fellow Christians and, beyond that, the whole Body of Christ. This must be an act of mercy and encouragement, not severity. Paul speaks from experience in this regard (2:11–16).

6:2 the law of Christ: The entire life of Jesus is the law of Christian living (Mt 11:29). It is summarized in the commandment of love (Jn 13:34–35) and calls us to carry the **burdens** of others as Christ did for us (1 Pet 2:24). Christian charity prohibits indifference toward our neighbor but encourages us instead to bear up with his weaknesses (Rom 15:1) and make his joys and sorrows our own (Rom 12:15; 1 Cor 12:26; CCC 1965–70).

6:4 test his own work: It is important to examine our lives before God and not to compare ourselves with others (2 Cor 13:5). In the end, everyone is responsible for his own actions and will give an account to the Lord (1 Cor 4:5).

6:6 share all good things: This probably refers to material and financial support that local congregations rightfully owe their spiritual leaders (Lk 10:7; 1 Cor 9:11–14).

6:7–9 The principle of sowing and reaping is an inflexible law of the spiritual life (Job 4:8; Jer 17:10). Just as farmers invariably harvest the same crop they planted, so every thought, word, and deed sown in this life has a consequence that springs

directly from it in the next. Those who sow in the **Spirit** will reap holiness and heavenly glory; those who sow in the **flesh** can expect nothing but death and decay. Since Paul speaks of a lifetime of **well-doing**, patience and perseverance are needed to see the fruit of our labors (Mt 24:13; Rom 2:6–7; Heb 3:14).

6:11 I am writing: Paul penned the postscript of Galatians himself, whereas the body of the letter was dictated to a secretary, as in Rom 16:22 and 2 Thess 3:17. He writes with **large letters** either for emphasis or because of poor eyesight (4:15).

6:12–13 The Judaizers were driven by fear of persecution, probably from Jewish nationalists who pressured them to make circumcision the focus of their missionary efforts. Paul accuses them of abandoning the true gospel, not out of conviction, but out of cowardice. See notes on 2:3 and 2:14.

6:14 crucified to me: Paul reiterates what he said in 2:20 and 5:24, that in Christ our sins and worldly passions are put to death. Paul thus emphasizes that the Cross—not circumcision—is the sign of our salvation (6:15; 1 Cor 1:18).

6:15 a new creation: The indwelling of the Spirit renews us from within and makes us sharers in the divine life (2 Pet 1:4; CCC 1214). The regenerating grace of the New Covenant will eventually permeate the entire cosmos (Rom 8:19–23; Rev 21:1). See note on 2 Cor 5:17.

6:16 Peace and mercy: For similar benedictions, see Ps 128:6 and Sir 50:22–23. **the Israel of God:** The covenant family of believing Israel united with the Gentiles. See essay: *Kingdom Restoration* at Acts 15.

6:17 the marks of Jesus: Property and slaves in the ancient world were branded with a mark of ownership. Paul views himself as a slave of Christ (Rom 1:1) who bears physical scars from the many persecutions that accompanied his apostolic work (Acts 14:19; 16:22; 2 Cor 11:23–29).

---

[1] Or *through whom.*

STUDY QUESTIONS
Galatians

Chapter 1

For understanding
1. **1:1–10.** What makes the opening of this letter different from those of most other Pauline letters? How is this difference corroborated by the contents of this letter?
2. **1:8.** In the Greek OT, what Hebrew term is the Greek *anathema* used to translate? What does the Hebrew word mean? How does the NT use the term? How does Paul use it here, and why?
3. **1:10.** What are the Judaizers accusing Paul of doing with the requirements of the original gospel? What does Paul accuse them of doing?
4. **1:18.** How soon did Paul travel to Jerusalem after he became a Christian? What does the Greek (not the English) wording indicate that he did during this time? Whom did Paul visit?

For application
1. **1:6–7.** How well do you know your Catholic faith? How committed to it are you? How willing would you be to defend your commitment to it if a non-Catholic evangelist were to try to "disprove" the Catholic understanding of the gospel?
2. **1:8–9.** Since even Catholic preachers, teachers, and theologians may differ in their view of what is authentic Church teaching, how is it possible to recognize whether they are preaching a "different gospel" or not? How often do you consult a trustworthy adult catechism to answer questions you may have about your faith?
3. **1:13–14.** If you were ever lukewarm about your faith, or even fell away from it for a while, how did you relate to friends or relatives who were still active? What brought you back to a serious practice of your faith?
4. **1:18.** Who has had the greatest influence on your understanding of the faith? What did that person (or those persons) do or say to make such an impact? How has that example influenced the way you encourage others?

Chapter 2

For understanding
1. **2:3.** What historical events in Jewish history provide a background for the expression "compelled to be circumcised"? How are the Judaizers acting in an analogous way?
2. **2:9.** What might be the reason Paul names James before Cephas (Peter) in this verse? What is James' position?
3. **Essay: Works of the Law.** What do several modern Scripture scholars think Paul was referring to in using this expression? How is this new understanding actually an old one? What is the theological meaning of these "works"?
4. **2:20.** To what did Paul die when he was "crucified" with Jesus? In what sacramental context does this union with Christ take place?

For application
1. **2:2.** If you teach others the faith, who oversees what you do? What is the link between your role as a catechist or teacher and those who represent the Magisterium?
2. **2:11–14.** When someone in authority over you acts in a way that appears inconsistent, insincere, or even morally dangerous, what do you do about it? When someone confronts you with such an accusation regarding your own conduct, how do you respond?
3. **2:15–21.** If one is not justified by works of the law, what is the point of the Church's Code of Canon Law and other religious precepts?

Chapter 3

For understanding
1. **3:15–18.** How does Israel's failure to keep the Mosaic covenant affect God's self-imposed obligation? What is the reason for this?
2. **3:19.** Why was the Torah inserted into history between the Abrahamic covenant and the New Covenant? Explain both reasons given in the note.
3. **3:20.** What does the fact that Moses is a mediator between God and the chosen people imply? How is the Abrahamic covenant different from the Mosaic covenant in this regard?
4. **Word Study: Custodian (3:24–25).** What was the role of a tutor in Hellenistic society? How does Paul apply this role to that of the Mosaic Law? What does the coming of Christ do to the function of the Law?

For application
1. **3:2–5.** How would you apply these verses to developments in your own life? Is it possible to have a life-changing experience of God through faith, only to end up as a good "keeper of the rules"?
2. **3:10.** Most rule books come with lists of consequences for infractions of the rules. How do you feel when you deliberately break a rule you know to be reasonable? What does it mean to say that, by breaking one rule, you break them all? What is the "curse" in that?
3. **3:23–25.** How do these verses reflect the normal process of growing up? If you are a parent, how do you know when it is time to relax certain forms of discipline? How does one grow from too narrow a focus on keeping rules and into a life of faith?

Chapter 4

For understanding
1. **Word Study: Adoption (4:5).** In what stages does adoption as a *process* take place, according to Paul? From what does divine adoption *result*? What is the main difference between Christ and the Christian?
2. **4:6.** Why does Paul say the Father sent the Spirit? What is the joint mission of the Son and the Spirit? With what does the Spirit fill us? What does the word "Abba" suggest about the Spirit's mission?
3. **4:8.** What does Paul mean by saying that the Galatians "did not know God"? How did the gospel change that situation?
4. **4:24–31.** How do Hagar and Sarah symbolize the Old and the New Covenants, respectively? What contrast is Paul setting up between the sons of the earthly Jerusalem and those of the heavenly Jerusalem?

For application
1. **4:1–7.** Have you ever received an inheritance? What made you an heir? What did inheriting money or property say about your relationship to the one who left it to you? What does it mean for you to inherit what God owns?
2. **4:10.** What do you think Paul might say of the Christian calendar, which includes feasts, solemnities, and penitential seasons? What is the purpose of Christian liturgical seasons? How is that purpose different from what Paul says about the Old Covenant calendar?
3. **4:17–19.** Why do the Christian media make much of a celebrity who adopts the Christian faith? What effects can the resulting publicity have for the Church? What is the danger in that kind of publicity for the celebrity?

Chapter 5

For understanding
1. **5:1.** Why does Paul regard the Mosaic Law and faith in Jesus Christ as mutually exclusive? What did the Council of Florence (1422) say about Jewish Christians observing Mosaic ceremonies as necessary for salvation? Why?
2. **5:13.** What is Christian freedom for? Why can the Christian who is free from sin in Baptism and from the Law through faith not simply go and do whatever he feels like? What would be the consequence of that kind of license?
3. **5:14.** What is the chief aim of the Torah, and who fulfilled it to perfection? What makes it possible for us to fulfill the Law's intention in our own lives?
4. **5:16–24.** What, according to Paul, is going on in the heart of every Christian? What is meant by "flesh", here? What are the consequences of following the flesh and (by contrast) of following the Spirit?

For application
1. **5:1–6.** Although modern Catholics are unlikely to be tempted to yield to the slavery of the Mosaic Law, scrupulous persons may look on disobeying any of the Church's disciplinary regulations as mortally sinful, whereas lax Catholics may blithely disregard all regulations with no qualms of conscience. What is your position? What really is necessary for salvation? What are the ramifications of that position for how you live your life as a faithful Catholic?
2. **5:16–22.** Think about the "works of the flesh" that Paul lists that have been problem areas in your own life or for others you have known. What other "works of the flesh" are there that Paul did not include in his list? How do people tend to "gratify the desires" of fallen nature in these areas? What does Paul say is the consequence for those who indulge themselves in these ways?
3. **5:22–23.** Read the note for v. 22. How have you seen the development of this "fruit" in your own life? If you do not think you are growing in holiness, what do you think is the reason? Would others agree?
4. **5:24.** What does this passage mean for you? How do you "crucify the flesh"?

Chapter 6

For understanding
1. **6:2.** What is "the law of Christ"? What does Christian charity prohibit, and to what does it encourage us?
2. **6:7–9.** To what does the principle of sowing and reaping apply? What do those who sow in the Spirit reap? What do those who sow in the flesh reap? When does the reaping take place?
3. **6:14.** In Christ, what happens to our sins? For Paul, what is the real sign of our salvation?
4. **6:17.** As a slave of Christ, what brand does Paul bear on himself?

For application
1. **6:1.** What do you typically do when you notice a fellow Christian engaged in a pattern of sinful behavior? According to this verse, what should you do? What does it mean for you to be "spiritual"? (Hint: Look at 5:22–23.)
2. **6:6.** How do you "share all good things" with those who instruct or pastor you? Is Paul encouraging merely financial sharing or something more? When was the last time you invited a priest or a missionary to your home for dinner? What kind of fellowship do you think the clergy in most parishes have with their parishioners?
3. **6:10.** To whom does Paul primarily urge you to do good? Why them?
4. **6:14.** How important to you is your relationship to the Cross of Christ? How is this manifested in the way you live? Has the Cross of Christ truly "crucified" the world to you and you to the world? In what ways does the world still exercise an influence on your daily life? (What is your understanding of the term *world* here? What does it mean for it to be "crucified"?)

INTRODUCTION TO THE
LETTER OF SAINT PAUL TO THE EPHESIANS

Author The author of Ephesians twice identifies himself as the Apostle Paul, once at the beginning of the letter (1:1) and once in the middle (3:1). This claim was universally accepted by the early Church and remained an unquestioned tradition until Erasmus of Rotterdam first raised doubts about it in the sixteenth century. Since then, many have either questioned or denied that Paul wrote Ephesians, alleging that the tone and style of the letter differ so markedly from Paul's undisputed letters that it could not have come from the same author. It is widely held today that Ephesians was written in Paul's name by a Pauline disciple who wished to honor the apostle by developing his doctrine and applying it to new situations in the Church.

Although the distinctiveness of Ephesians among the letters of Paul should not be minimized or overlooked, it need not imply that Paul was not the author. Stylistic differences between Ephesians and Paul's other letters can largely be explained by the circumstances of his readers. No doubt Paul writes with a more terse and aggressive style in his other epistles, where he is wrestling with doctrinal and moral problems that plagued his missionary churches. His Ephesian readers, however, were not entrenched in controversy at this time, so it is not surprising that this letter has a more calm and lyrical style than is found elsewhere in Paul's writings. Claims that theological differences set Ephesians apart from the genuine Pauline writings are likewise overdrawn, since the presence of numerous Pauline ideas in the letter is precisely what leads scholars to insist that it must have been written by one of Paul's disciples. If anything, the NT collection of Paul's letters shows him to be an exceptionally versatile writer who can adapt both his manner and his message to the needs of his audience. It is important, therefore, not to exaggerate the uniqueness of Ephesians at the expense of other factors that cohere nicely with the traditional view.

Date The question of when Ephesians was written depends upon the prior question of authorship. Supporters of Pauline authorship naturally date the letter within the time frame of the apostle's ministry. Most correlate the imprisonment mentioned in 3:1, 4:1, and 6:20 with Paul's first imprisonment in Rome, where he lived under house arrest from A.D. 60 to 62, awaiting trial before the tribunal of Caesar (Acts 28:16, 30). This would imply a date for Ephesians in the early 60s alongside Paul's other "Captivity Epistles": Philippians (Phil 1:12–14), Colossians (4:3), and Philemon (Philem 9). Scholars

who contend the letter was written by one of Paul's admirers date it as late as the 90s, long after the apostle's martyrdom in the mid 60s.

Destination The intended readership of Ephesians is more difficult to establish than it first appears. This is because the textual tradition underlying the letter's opening verse is uncertain: the words "in Ephesus" are missing from some of the most ancient manuscripts of the epistle in existence and, for this reason, may have been added *after* the letter was originally written (see textual note *a* on Eph 1:1). Identification of the readers thus depends on whether or not the disputed words are original. (1) If the phrase "in Ephesus" is authentic, then Paul was writing to Christians in the leading metropolis of the Roman province of Asia (southwest Turkey). This would not be surprising, as Paul spent several years ministering to the Ephesians and disseminating the gospel throughout the region (Acts 19:1–10; 20:31). (2) If the phrase was not part of the original letter, as many scholars maintain, then it seems the intended audience was more general than specific. Advocates of this position often describe Ephesians as a circular letter that Paul intended for several churches in Asia Minor. In this case, the Church at Ephesus was probably only one of several churches he expected to receive the letter.

Themes and Characteristics Ephesians sets before us a vision of Christ *reigning* in heaven next to the Father (1:20) and *renewing* the earth through his Church (3:10). Though Paul often attacks doctrinal error and moral laxity in his letters, he seizes the opportunity in Ephesians to step back from these controversies to contemplate and articulate in a more reflective way God's saving work in Jesus. Instead of pastoral surgery, then, Paul gives the Ephesians a dose of preventative medicine, hoping that a deeper appreciation of God's blessings will lead them to a more mature commitment to the gospel. Since many of Paul's readers are recent converts, Ephesians might best be described as Paul's mystagogical catechesis for the newly baptized.

The towering theme of Ephesians is the "mystery" of Jesus Christ once concealed but now revealed (1:9; 3:4, 9). This is first of all the mystery of Christ the Redeemer, whose violent death on the Cross was a vicarious sacrifice for the redemption of Israel and the Gentiles alike (1:7; 2:16; 5:2). Having died to restore peace between the Father and

the human family, Christ now reigns supreme over all things at the right hand of the Father in heaven (1:20). So far is he exalted above creation that even the angels find themselves under his feet (1:21–22). As Paul reflects upon these redeeming achievements of Christ, he is not content to view them as events confined to the past. Rather, the Resurrection, Ascension, and Enthronement of Christ are saving mysteries that continue to grace our lives and souls in the present, making us participants in his royal, priestly, and prophetic mission to the world (2:4–6; 5:2).

The mystery of Christ is also the mystery of his ecclesial body, the Church. Nowhere does Paul give a more majestic presentation of this truth than in Ephesians. The Church he describes is nothing less than God's new creation in Christ (2:10, 15; 2 Cor 5:17). She is a holy and universal community that shines out to a world shattered by sin. Her life comes from the divine Trinity, as her members are made the children of the Father (1:5), the body and bride of the Son (5:22–32), and the temple of the Holy Spirit (2:21–22). Her dimensions are international, as she gathers together all peoples and nations into the family of the New Covenant (2:11–22; 3:4–6). The grace that unites the Church with her Lord is the grace of being "in Christ" (1:3, 7, 10, 13). This union between Christ in his glorified body and Christ in his mystical body was first revealed to Paul at his conversion (Acts 9:3–5). Now, after many years of preaching and meditation, he is able to explain its heights and depths in simple yet profound terms for those newly acquainted with the gospel.

OUTLINE OF THE LETTER OF SAINT PAUL TO THE EPHESIANS

1. **Opening Address (1:1–2)**

2. **Doctrinal Exposition (1:3—3:21)**
    A.   Divine Origin of the Church (1:3–14)
    B.   Prayer for the Church (1:15–23)
    C.   Building Up the Church (2:1–22)
    D.   Mystery of the Church (3:1–13)
    E.   Prayer for the Church (3:14–21)

3. **Moral Exhortation (4:1—6:20)**
    A.   Unity of the Church (4:1–16)
    B.   Moral Maturity in the Church (4:17—5:20)
    C.   Household Life in the Church (5:21—6:9)
    D.   Spiritual Warfare in the Church (6:10–20)

4. **Closing Farewell (6:21–24)**

THE LETTER OF SAINT PAUL TO THE
EPHESIANS

Salutation

1 Paul, an apostle of Christ Jesus by the will of God,

To the saints who are also faithful[a] in Christ Jesus:

2 Grace to you and peace from God our Father and the Lord Jesus Christ.

Spiritual Blessings in Christ

3 Blessed be the God and Father of our Lord Jesus Christ, who has blessed us in Christ with every spiritual blessing in the heavenly places, [4]even as he chose us in him before the foundation of the world, that we should be holy and blameless before him. [5]He destined us in love[b] to be his sons through Jesus Christ, according to the purpose of his will, [6]to the praise of his glorious grace which he freely bestowed on us in the Beloved. [7]In him we have redemption through his blood, the forgiveness of our trespasses, according to the riches of his grace [8]which he lavished upon us. [9]For he has made known to us in all wisdom and insight the mystery of his will, according to his purpose which he set forth in Christ [10]as a plan for the fulness of time, to unite all things in him, things in heaven and things on earth.

11 In him, according to the purpose of him who accomplishes all things according to the counsel of his will, [12]we who first hoped in Christ have been

---

1:3: 2 Cor 1:3.   **1:6:** Col 1:13.   **1:7:** Col 1:14.   **1:10:** Gal 4:4.

1:1 Paul: Named as the sender of the letter. For a discussion of Pauline authorship, see introduction: *Author* and notes on 3:8 and 6:20. **apostle of Christ:** Paul was formally commissioned by Jesus to carry the gospel to "the Gentiles" and "the sons of Israel" (Acts 9:15; Rom 11:13–14). **the saints:** I.e., those who are baptized and set apart to serve God (1 Cor 6:11). The majority of surviving manuscripts include the words "in Ephesus" in this verse, but they are lacking in some of the most ancient copies of the letter we possess (see textual note a). For the implications of this, see introduction: *Destination*.

1:2 Grace . . . and peace: A customary greeting in Paul's letters (Rom 1:7; 1 Cor 1:3; Gal 1:3).

📖 **1:3–14** A panoramic view of salvation that stretches from the past (election, 1:4) to the present (adoption, 1:5) to the future (recapitulation, 1:10). Like an orchestral overture, it introduces many themes to be developed in subsequent chapters. Structurally, Paul has organized this benediction around the work of the Trinity (CCC 257–58). The Father chooses us (1:4), the Son redeems us (1:7), and the Holy Spirit seals us (1:13). Notice, too, that Paul celebrates blessings traditionally linked with Baptism, such as sonship (1:5), grace (1:6), forgiveness (1:7), and sealing (1:13). These 12 verses comprise only one sentence in the original Greek. ● Paul's benediction follows the format of a Hebrew *berakah*, i.e., a prayer of blessing and praise to God in elevated language (1 Chron 29:10–13; Tob 13:1–18; Dan 3:3–68) (CCC 1078, 2627).

1:2 Father: The preeminent title for God in Ephesians (1:3, 17; 2:18; 3:14; 4:6; 5:20; 6:23).

1:3 in Christ: A description of our union with Jesus through grace. Similar expressions of incorporation punctuate the letter and culminate in Paul's vision of Christ as the "head" of his mystical "body", the Church (1:22–23; 2:16; 5:23). **the heavenly places:** I.e., the spiritual realm where believers sit enthroned with Christ (1:20; 2:6) and where angels and demons move about unseen (3:10; 6:12). See note on 2:6.

📖 **1:4 holy and blameless:** The standard of spiritual perfection that God desires for his children (5:27; Col 1:22).

● Paul employs cultic terminology from the OT, where holy means "set apart" for the Lord and blameless means "unblemished" or "fit for sacrifice". This recalls how animals were set apart for priestly inspection, and only those free of physical defects could be sacrificed to Yahweh (Lev 1:3, 10). These offerings were mere shadows of the Christian vocation to offer ourselves as holy and living sacrifices to the Father (Rom 12:1) (CCC 1426, 2807). See note on 5:2.

⚜ **1:5 He destined us:** The Father predestined believers for divine adoption (1:4). This eternal decree springs from his love and unfolds in history as the elect are saved by grace (Gal 4:5) and eventually brought to glory (Rom 8:23). Because the doctrine of predestination holds together two mysteries, one of divine sovereignty and one of human freedom, it should be an incentive for Christians to confirm their election through works of righteousness (2 Pet 1:10), rather than an excuse for spiritual indifference or moral laxity. We cannot gain access to God's hidden *plan*, but we do know the *precepts* he has revealed for our salvation (Deut 29:29). As with the election of Israel, God took no consideration of our merits or worthiness when he predestined our adoption in Christ (Deut 7:7; Rom 9:10–11) (CCC 381, 600). See note on Rom 8:29. ● Predestination can have no other cause than the will of God alone. And the sole motive for God's predestinating will is to communicate his divine goodness to others (St. Thomas Aquinas, *Commentary on Ephesians* 1, 1).

📖 **1:7 redemption:** Freedom purchased for a slave or prisoner by a ransom price. Christ redeemed us *from* sin and *for* divine sonship (Gal 4:5) at the expense of his own blood (Rev 5:9; CCC 517). ● Divine redemption is first displayed in the Bible in the Exodus (Ex 15:13; Deut 7:8). We participate in a new and spiritual Exodus when Christ rescues us from the bondage of guilt and the tyranny of the devil (Rom 6:15–18).

1:9 the mystery: A central theme in Ephesians, introduced here and developed more fully in 3:1–19. See word study: *Mystery* at Eph 3:3.

1:12–13 Here and elsewhere Paul alternates between **we** and **you**. Among the options, (1) "we" could refer to Jewish Christians (us, 2:14), and "you" to Gentile Christians (2:11); or

---

[a] Other ancient authorities read *who are at Ephesus and faithful*.
[b] Or *before him in love, having destined us*.

destined and appointed to live for the praise of his glory. [13]In him you also, who have heard the word of truth, the gospel of your salvation, and have believed in him, were sealed with the promised Holy Spirit, [14]who is the guarantee of our inheritance until we acquire possession of it, to the praise of his glory.

Paul's Prayer

15 For this reason, because I have heard of your faith in the Lord Jesus and your love [c] toward all the saints, [16]I do not cease to give thanks for you, remembering you in my prayers, [17]that the God of our Lord Jesus Christ, the Father of glory, may give

you a spirit of wisdom and of revelation in the knowledge of him, [18]having the eyes of your hearts enlightened, that you may know what is the hope to which he has called you, what are the riches of his glorious inheritance in the saints, [19]and what is the immeasurable greatness of his power in us who believe, according to the working of his great might [20]which he accomplished in Christ when he raised him from the dead and made him sit at his right hand in the heavenly places, [21]far above all rule and authority and power and dominion, and above every name that is named, not only in this age but also in that which is to come; [22]and he has put all

---

1:14: 2 Cor 1:22.   **1:15:** Col 1:9.   **1:16:** Col 1:3.   **1:18:** Deut 33:3.   **1:20:** Ps 110:1.
1:21: Col 1:6; 2:10, 15.   **1:22:** Ps 8:6; Col 1:19.

---

(2) "we" may refer to Christians known by Paul, and "you" to those unacquainted with Paul personally (1:15; 3:2); or (3) "we" might refer to believers long since converted (1:12), and "you" to more recent converts. None of these possibilities is mutually exclusive of another, so it is quite possible the groups in question fall into more than one category.

1:13 sealed: In the ancient world, seals were marks of ownership and protection (4:30; Ezek 9:4–6; Rev 7:4). Believers are divinely sealed by the Spirit. The Church Fathers employed this language to describe the indelible mark impressed upon the soul in Baptism, Confirmation, and Holy Orders (CCC 698, 1272–74, 1296). See note on 2 Cor 1:22. ● In Pauline theology, Baptism does to the soul what circumcision did to body: it marks it with the sign and seal of the covenant (Rom 4:11). See note on Col 2:11.

---

[c] Other ancient authorities omit *your love*.

Word Study

Unite (Eph 1:10)

Anakephalaioō (Gk.): "recapitulate" or "sum up under one head". The verb is rarely used in antiquity and appears only twice in the NT. It can refer to the placement of a numeric sum over a list of figures that have been added or, more generally, to a gathering together of scattered elements. In Rom 13:9, Paul uses this Greek word to explain how the moral commandments of the Law all add up to one: "You shall love your neighbor as yourself." In Eph 1:10, he asserts that God's supreme plan for the universe is to put Jesus Christ at the summit of all things seen and unseen. Present in the background is Adam, whose headship over the human family left the world in a state of chaos and sin. Christ comes as the new Adam to be established as the new "head" over all things (Eph 1:22; see also 5:23). He reverses the damage done by Adam's rebellion by piecing creation back together again and by summoning a family reunion of all God's children: Israel, the Gentiles, and even the angels. This grand work of reunification is already under way and will continue until Christ subdues his enemies (1 Cor 15:24–28) and the grace of redemption permeates the entire universe (Rom 8:19–23) (CCC 518, 1042–43).

1:14 guarantee: An expression derived from a Hebrew term meaning "pledge" or "down payment" (Gen 38:17–18). The Spirit received in Baptism (Acts 2:38) is thus a first installment of the fullness of God's life and blessing we hope to possess in heaven (2 Cor 1:22; 5:5; CCC 1107).

1:15 I have heard: The comment here and at 4:21 suggests that Paul has never met his intended readers in person.

1:18 your hearts: In biblical thinking, the heart is the center of the person, where thinking, willing, and feeling originate. See word study: *Heart* at Deut 30:6. **enlightened:** By the grace of faith in Christ (5:14). Early theologians described Baptism as the sacrament of "enlightenment" (CCC 1216).

1:20 sit at his right hand: A position of royal honor and sovereignty. ● Paul alludes to Ps 110:1, which describes the coronation and enthronement of the Messiah in heaven. Now reigning beside the Father, Christ wields authority to govern the cosmos (Mk 16:19; CCC 668). Psalm 110 is the most frequently cited passage of the OT in the NT (Mt 22:44; Acts 2:34–35; 1 Cor 15:25; Heb 1:13).

1:21 rule and authority and power: Names given in Jewish and Christian tradition to different choirs or orders of angels. They can refer to blessed angels or to demons who fell from their ranks (3:10; 6:12; Col 2:15; 1 Pet 3:22). Paul's point is that God has elevated Christ far above all creation, including things visible and material as well as things invisible and spiritual (Col 1:16; CCC 331–36, 395). ● Catholic theologians have traditionally recognized nine choirs of angels arranged in three levels or hierarchies. The first consists of the Seraphim, Cherubim, and Thrones; the second of the Dominions, Authorities, and Powers; and the third of the Rulers, Archangels, and common Angels. Theologians classify these angelic orders according to their divinely given tasks. **this age:** Jewish tradition distinguished between the *present* evil age and the *coming* messianic age. Just as Christ's coming marked the transition from Old Covenant era to the New, so he will come again in glory to close the present age of history and open the future age of eternity (Mk 10:30; Lk 20:34–36).

1:22 under his feet: An indication of subjection and defeat. ● Paul alludes to Ps 8:6, where David marvels that God crowned Adam and his descendants as rulers of his creation (Gen 1:26). Although this government was frustrated because of sin, Jesus reclaims Adam's dominion over the visible world and extends it over the angelic realms as well (Heb 2:5–9). All will acknowledge Christ's kingship when he subdues his last remaining enemies—the devil, the demons, and death. See note on 1 Cor 15:25–27. ● It is an awesome fact that the whole power of creation will bow before a man, in whom is the divine Word (St. John Chrysostom, *Homilies on Ephesians* 3, 1). **the head:** Christ reigns supreme over the cosmos and the universal Church, which is his "body" (1:23). See word study: *Head* at Eph 5:23. ● God has set over all creation one and the same head, the incarnate Christ. That is, he has

things under his feet and has made him the head over all things for the Church, [23]which is his body, the fulness of him who fills all in all.

From Death to Life with Christ

2 And you he made alive, when you were dead through the trespasses and sins [2]in which you once walked, following the course of this world, following the prince of the power of the air, the spirit that is now at work in the sons of disobedience. [3]Among these we all once lived in the passions of our flesh, following the desires of body and mind, and so we were by nature children of wrath, like the rest of mankind. [4]But God, who is rich in mercy, out of the great love with which he loved us, [5]even when we were dead through our trespasses, made us alive together with Christ (by grace you have been saved), [6]and raised us up with him, and made us sit with him in the heavenly places in Christ Jesus, [7]that in the coming ages he might show the immeasurable riches of his grace in kindness toward us in Christ Jesus. [8]For by grace you have been saved through faith; and this is not your own doing, it is the gift of God—[9]not because of works, lest any man should boast. [10]For we are his workmanship, created in Christ Jesus for good works, which God prepared beforehand, that we should walk in them.

One in Christ

11 Therefore remember that at one time you Gentiles in the flesh, called the uncircumcision by what is called the circumcision, which is made in the flesh by hands—[12]remember that you were at that time separated from Christ, alienated from the commonwealth of Israel, and strangers to the covenants of promise, having no hope and without God in the world. [13]But now in Christ Jesus you who once were far off have been brought near in the blood of Christ. [14]For he is our peace, who has made us both one, and has broken down the dividing wall of hostility, [15]by abolishing in his flesh the law of commandments and ordinances, that he might create in himself one new man in place of the two, so making peace, [16]and might reconcile us

---

1:23: Rom 12:5; Col 2:17.   2:2: Col 1:13.   2:8: Gal 2:16.   2:12: Is 57:19.

---

given to angels and men one and the same government (St. John Chrysostom, *Homilies on Ephesians* 1, 1).

2:1–22 A tragic picture of man without God. The chapter falls into two halves: the first explains how Christ reconciles men with God (2:1-10), and the second how Christ reconciles men and nations with one another (2:11-22). Notice that Paul stresses the radical difference between living "by grace" (2:5) and living "by nature" (2:3).

2:1 you were dead: Spiritual death is the consequence of sin (Rom 5:12), and those who are dead in sin cannot recover the life and grace of God for themselves any more than a corpse can revive itself to live again. Believers are brought from spiritual death to spiritual life through Baptism (2:5; Jn 5:24; Rom 6:4, 23).

2:2 power of the air: Paul assumes the ancient belief that demonic spirits crowd the atmosphere, posing an ominous and ongoing threat to our spiritual lives. The **prince** among them is Satan, the archenemy of God, who is veiled from our sight but is not thereby any less real or dangerous (4:27; 6:11; Jn 8:44). Man is powerless to resist the domination of the devil without the assistance of grace (6:11-17). See note on 6:10-17. **sons of disobedience:** A Hebraism meaning "rebels" or "sinners" (5:6).

✠ **2:3 children of wrath:** I.e., enemies of God liable to judgment. This results (1) from the dismal inheritance of Original Sin, which spreads to every living person by natural generation (by nature, 2:3), and (2) from the actual sins and ongoing rebellion of the human family against God (trespasses and sins, 2:1) (CCC 402-5). See note on Rom 5:12. ● Through the sin of the first man, which came from his free will, our nature became corrupted and ruined; and nothing but the grace of God alone restores it (St. Augustine, *On the Grace of Christ* 55).

2:5-6 By grace we share in the exaltation of Christ: his rising from the dead, his ascent into heaven, and his enthronement at the Father's right hand. Paul articulates this theology of participation by using the preposition **with** three times in these verses (in Greek, the verbal prefix *syn-*).

2:6 sit with him: I.e., we are made to share in the heavenly reign of Christ (CCC 1003).

2:8 grace: The biblical term for (1) God's favor and (2) God's supernatural life. The former designates the *conditions* of its bestowal (a free and undeserved gift, Rom 6:23), and the latter designates the *content* of the gift we receive (a share in the

divine nature, 2 Pet 1:4) (CCC 1996-2003). **have been saved:** Salvation is here described as a present state resulting from a past action. The preceding context indicates that deliverance from sin and spiritual death is in view (2:1-3). That salvation is not thereby assured but is also a future hope, see note on Rom 5:10. **through faith:** Faith is instrumental in saving us and uniting us with Christ. In the context of conversion, salvation is *conferred* through the instrument of Baptism (1 Pet 3:21), and salvation is *received* through the instrument of faith (Rom 3:24-25). For Paul, belief in Jesus Christ is a divine gift (Phil 1:29) that we exercise when we adhere to God with trust (personal aspect) and assent to the truth he has revealed in the gospel (propositional aspect) (CCC 177).

2:9 lest any . . . boast: Because salvation is neither a payment for services rendered nor a personal achievement, there is no room for pride or boasting on our part (1 Cor 4:7).

✠ **2:10 good works:** Works of righteousness that pertain to salvation (Rom 2:6-7). These are made possible by the grace of God empowering us from within (Phil 2:12-13; Heb 13:20-21). ● The Second Council of Orange decreed in A.D. 529 that man, weakened by the Fall of Adam, is incapable of performing works worthy of eternal life by his own natural strength. Only by the supernatural help of the Spirit can we be humble, obedient, and loving in a way that truly pleases the Lord (*Canons* 1-25) (CCC 2008-11).

2:11 the uncircumcision: A Jewish epithet for Gentiles, who were excluded from the covenant and blessings God gave to Israel in ages past (2:12; Rom 9:4-5). **in the flesh:** Circumcision of the foreskin was a procedure done by human hands as a sign of the Abrahamic covenant (Gen 17:9-14). This is in contrast to the circumcision of the heart, which Christ performs without human hands in the waters of Baptism (Rom 2:28-29; Col 2:11-12).

2:14 he is our peace: The peace of Christ is not worldly tranquillity but a spiritual peace rooted in our reconciliation with the Father (Jn 14:27; Rom 5:1; CCC 2305). See word study: *Peace* at Col 3:15. **dividing wall:** Paul alludes to a wall in the Jerusalem Temple that separated the outer court of the Gentiles from the inner courts, where Israel alone could pray and sacrifice. Gates leading into the inner precincts were posted with signs warning that Gentile trespassers would face the death penalty. For Paul, this wall of separation represents the OT theology of separation that required Israel to insulate itself from the idolatry and immorality of the nations (Lev 20:26). Christ

both to God in one body through the cross, thereby bringing the hostility to an end. [17]And he came and preached peace to you who were far off and peace to those who were near; [18]for through him we both have access in one Spirit to the Father. [19]So then you are no longer strangers and sojourners, but you are fellow citizens with the saints and members of the household of God, [20]built upon the foundation of the apostles and prophets, Christ Jesus himself being the cornerstone, [21]in whom the whole structure is joined together and grows into a holy temple in the Lord; [22]in whom you also are built into it for a dwelling place of God in the Spirit.

Paul's Ministry to the Gentiles

3 For this reason I, Paul, a prisoner for Christ Jesus on behalf of you Gentiles—[2]assuming that you have heard of the stewardship of God's grace that was given to me for you, [3]how the mystery was made known to me by revelation, as I have written briefly. [4]When you read this you can perceive my insight into the mystery of Christ, [5]which was not made known to the sons of men in other generations as it has now been revealed to his holy apostles and prophets by the Spirit; [6]that is, how the Gentiles are fellow heirs, members of the same body, and partakers of the promise in Christ Jesus through the gospel.

7 Of this gospel I was made a minister according to the gift of God's grace which was given me by the working of his power. [8]To me, though I am the very least of all the saints, this grace was given, to preach to the Gentiles the unsearchable riches of Christ, [9]and to make all men see what is the plan of

---

2:17: Is 57:19. **3:2:** Col 1:25. **3:6:** Col 1:27. **3:9:** Col 1:26.

---

dismantled this barricade when, having fulfilled the Law to perfection, he abolished the legal precepts (2:15) that set Israel apart from the Gentiles (e.g., circumcision, animal sacrifice, dietary laws, festival days). As a result, the age when Jew and Gentile were divided has given way to the messianic age, when all nations are united in Christ (Rom 15:7–12; Gal 3:28).

2:17 far off . . . near: Signifies spiritual distance from God. ● Paul is paraphrasing Is 57:19, where peace is proclaimed both to Israel, the people nearest the Lord, and to the Gentiles, the people of distant lands who once lived far from God.

2:18 access: The way to the Father passes through Christ (3:11–12). Perhaps Paul is contrasting Jesus with the veil of the Temple, which, in the old economy, greatly restricted access to the Lord. The interpretation is not certain, but Temple imagery fills the surrounding context, and elsewhere links are forged

between Christ and the sanctuary veil (Mk 15:37–38; Heb 10:19–20).

2:19 members: I.e., family members by virtue of divine adoption (1:5; Gal 4:5).

2:20 apostles and prophets: The foundation stones of the universal Church, here viewed as a spiritual temple (1 Pet 2:4–8). Both fulfilled the unrepeatable mission of establishing Christ's kingdom in the world for all time. For other references to NT prophets, see 4:11, Acts 13:1, and 1 Cor 12:28 (see also CCC 857). **cornerstone:** The first stone set in place when beginning construction on a new building, in this case a temple. It served as the square to line up the rest of the structure and was part of the foundation at the base of the edifice. The honored position of the cornerstone is a fitting description of Christ's role as the immovable foundation of the Church (1 Cor 3:11). Some prefer to visualize Christ as the keystone that holds together a Roman archway, but cornerstones are generally foundation stones in Semitic architecture (Job 38:6; Jer 51:26). ● The term used here for cornerstone is found only in Is 28:16 in the Greek OT. Jewish tradition expressed in the Aramaic *Targum of Isaiah* viewed this stone as a symbol of the messianic "king" of Israel.

2:21 a holy temple: The Church is a spiritual sanctuary that is living and inclusive. Its foundation is Christ, his apostles, and the early Christian prophets (2:20); its walls are believers from every nation fitted and bonded together by grace (2:22); and its holiness comes from the sanctifying presence of the Spirit who dwells within (2:22) (CCC 756, 797).

3:1 Paul, a prisoner: Probably in Rome, possibly under house arrest (Acts 28:16, 30).

3:2 stewardship: The administrative tasks of a servant in charge of the household and finances of his master. Paul is a steward of divine mysteries (1 Cor 4:1) chosen to manage the household affairs of the Church (1 Tim 3:15). The grace of God has come to him on its way to others—the "Gentiles" and the "sons of Israel" (Acts 9:15).

3:3 written briefly: Points back to earlier comments about the mystery revealed in Christ (1:9–10) and the salvation of the Gentiles (2:11–22).

3:6 Gentiles are fellow heirs: The OT revealed *that* the nations would be blessed, but it remained unclear *how* this would take place (Gen 22:16–18; Sir 44:21; Is 49:6; Zech 2:11). It was also not clear before the proclamation of the gospel whether the Gentiles would be saved on an equal footing with Israel (Gal 3:28; Col 3:11).

3:8 I am the very least: Paul is overcome by a sense of unworthiness and overawed that God could transform a sinner like himself into a servant of the gospel (1 Cor 15:9; 1 Tim 1:15).

Word Study

Mystery (Eph 3:3)

Mystērion (Gk.): "mystery" or "secret". The term is used six times in Ephesians and 22 times in the rest of the NT. Like Jesus, who revealed the mysteries of his kingdom through parables (Mt 13:11; Mk 4:11), Paul often teaches his readers about the hidden plan of God now manifest in the reign of Christ (Rom 16:25; 1 Cor 15:51; Eph 5:32; Col 2:2; 1 Tim 3:16). The most likely background for this notion is the Book of Daniel, where "mystery" (Aramaic *raz*) appears eight times in a single chapter (Dan 2:18–19, 27–30, 47). Here the mystery is described in a dream to the Babylonian king Nebuchadnezzar, who envisioned a huge statue of a human body that symbolized the great empires of the earth. Though the king himself was the "head" (Dan 2:38) of the statue who received his empire from the Lord (Dan 2:37), Daniel went on to describe how the statue would be destroyed and replaced by the messianic kingdom of God. This is the mystery of the kingdom revealed in Ephesians (Eph 1:9; 3:4, 9). It is the mystery of another body, the Church, with its head, Jesus Christ (CCC 772, 1066).

the mystery hidden for ages in [d] God who created all things; [10]that through the Church the manifold wisdom of God might now be made known to the principalities and powers in the heavenly places. [11]This was according to the eternal purpose which he has realized in Christ Jesus our Lord, [12]in whom we have boldness and confidence of access through our faith in him. [13]So I ask you not to [e] lose heart over what I am suffering for you, which is your glory.

Prayer for the Ephesians

14 For this reason I bow my knees before the Father, [15]from whom every family in heaven and on earth is named, [16]that according to the riches of his glory he may grant you to be strengthened with might through his Spirit in the inner man, [17]and that Christ may dwell in your hearts through faith; that you, being rooted and grounded in love, [18]may have power to comprehend with all the saints what is the breadth and length and height and depth, [19]and to know the love of Christ which surpasses knowledge, that you may be filled with all the fulness of God.

20 Now to him who by the power at work within us is able to do far more abundantly than all that we ask or think, [21]to him be glory in the Church and in Christ Jesus to all generations, for ever and ever. Amen.

Unity in the Body of Christ

4 I therefore, a prisoner for the Lord, beg you to walk in a manner worthy of the calling to which you have been called, [2]with all lowliness and meekness, with patience, forbearing one another in love, [3]eager to maintain the unity of the Spirit in the bond of peace. [4]There is one body and one Spirit, just as you were called to the one hope that belongs to your call, [5]one Lord, one faith, one baptism, [6]one God and Father of us all, who is above all and through all and in all. [7]But grace was given to each of us according to the measure of Christ's gift. [8]Therefore it is said,

"When he ascended on high he led a host of captives,

and he gave gifts to men."

[9](In saying, "He ascended," what does it mean but that he had also descended into the lower parts of

---

4:2: Col 3:12–13.   **4:8:** Ps 68:18.

3:10 through the Church: Christ continues to teach, heal, and save the world through his mystical body. This mystery was once hidden from the angels (1 Pet 1:12) but is now manifest for the principalities and powers to look on and learn the plan of salvation. To the blessed angels, it is a glorious vision of an ever-expanding family; to the demons, it is a frightful spectacle of their own achievements toppling over with the triumph of the gospel. Elsewhere Paul portrays the Church as a pillar that upholds the truth for all to see (1 Tim 3:15). See note on 1:21.

3:14 bow my knees: Kneeling is a gesture of submission and worship (Ps 95:6; Acts 20:36). It is a way of expressing through the body the inner attitude of the heart (CCC 2702–3).

3:15 family: The term (Gk. *patria*) refers to a group of related individuals who trace their origin to a common father or forefather and is linguistically related to the word "Father" (Gk. *patēr*) in the preceding verse. Because God is the supreme Father of men and angels, his life-giving Paternity is the reality of which created fatherhood and family life are only a reflection (CCC 239, 2214).

3:18 breadth . . . length . . . height . . . depth: Many connect these dimensions with the limitless scope of Christ's love, which surpasses understanding (3:19). Others see a reference to the untraceable vastness of God and his wisdom (Job 11:7–9) or to the cubic proportions of the heavenly Jerusalem (Rev 21:16). ● The four dimensions are the four extensions of the Cross. By height is meant heaven, by depth the underworld, by length and breadth the cosmic order in between. In each of these realms, devotion to the Lord is rendered (St. Gregory of Nyssa, *On the Three Days*).

3:20 more abundantly: God can accomplish things far beyond expectation if only we pray with faith (Jas 1:6–8) and remove from our lives the hindrances of sin (Ps 66:18; 1 Pet 3:7).

4:1–6:20 Paul completes his doctrinal exposition (chaps. 1–3) with moral exhortation (chaps. 4–6). The first half of the letter thus works in tandem with the second, showing how the standards of Christian belief are inseparable from the standards of Christian behavior (CCC 1971).

4:3 unity of the Spirit: The towering theme of 4:1–16 and of the letter in general. Because believers are baptized into one body (1 Cor 12:13), their union is displayed in the oneness of their faith (creed), life (code), and sacramental worship (cult). The Church is equipped to preserve this unity through the hierarchical leadership appointed by Christ (4:11–12). Paul's vision of a unified Church mirrors that of Jesus in Jn 17:6–26 (CCC 172–73, 814).

4:7 given to each: Every baptized believer is given spiritual gifts or charisms to be exercised for the good of the Church (1 Cor 12:4–11; 1 Pet 4:10). In this context, Paul focuses on the varied graces connected with ecclesiastical offices (4:11) (CCC 913).

4:8 When he ascended: A reference to Ps 68:18. Although the wording of Paul's citation differs from both the Hebrew and Greek versions of this text known to us, it approximates other renditions of the psalm in Aramaic and Syriac. ● Psalm 68 celebrates the triumphal procession of biblical history, when Israel, filing out of Egypt behind Yahweh, was led on its march to the summit of Mt. Zion in Jerusalem. The victories won by the Lord along the way earned him the right to distribute gifts and spoils of war to the Israelites. For Paul, the psalm points forward to the ascent of Jesus into the heavenly Jerusalem after disarming the forces of evil on the Cross (Col 2:15). The Church began to share in this victory when Christ poured out the gifts of the Spirit on Pentecost (Acts 2:33).

4:9–10 A parenthetical explanation of how Jesus fulfills Ps 68. Interpretations differ over the meaning of **lower parts of the earth.** (1) Some view this expression as a reference to earth itself, to which Christ descended in his Incarnation (Jn 3:13). (2) Others take it to mean the underworld, to which Jesus descended on Holy Saturday before rising again on Easter Sunday. The second view is more likely correct in light of similar expressions in the Greek versions of Ps 63:9 and 139:15 that clearly refer to the underworld of the dead. In this case, Paul is stressing that Christ has charted the extremities of the cosmos, descending to its deepest depths in his Passion and rising above its highest heights at his Ascension. This is not simply a journey through space; rather, it is an expression of Christ's supreme humiliation and exaltation. ● Several Church Fathers connected this verse with Christ's descent to the dead,

---

[d] Or *by.*

[e] Or *I ask that I may not.*

the earth? [10]He who descended is he who also ascended far above all the heavens, that he might fill all things.) [11]And his gifts were that some should be apostles, some prophets, some evangelists, some pastors and teachers, [12]to equip the saints for the work of ministry, for building up the body of Christ, [13]until we all attain to the unity of the faith and of the knowledge of the Son of God, to mature manhood, to the measure of the stature of the fulness of Christ; [14]so that we may no longer be children, tossed back and forth and carried about with every wind of doctrine, by the cunning of men, by their craftiness in deceitful wiles. [15]Rather, speaking the truth in love, we are to grow up in every way into him who is the head, into Christ, [16]from whom the whole body, joined and knit together by every joint with which it is supplied, when each part is work-

ing properly, makes bodily growth and upbuilds itself in love.

The Old Life and the New

17 Now this I affirm and testify in the Lord, that you must no longer walk as the Gentiles walk, in the futility of their minds; [18]they are darkened in their understanding, alienated from the life of God because of the ignorance that is in them, due to their hardness of heart; [19]they have become callous and have given themselves up to licentiousness, greedy to practice every kind of uncleanness. [20]You did not so learn Christ! —[21]assuming that you have heard about him and were taught in him, as the truth is in Jesus. [22]Put off the old man that belongs to your former manner of life and is corrupt through deceitful lusts, [23]and be renewed in the spirit of your minds, [24]and put on the new man,

---

4:15: Col 1:18.   4:16: Col 2:19.

---

in which he released the captive souls of the righteous and led them up to heaven (1 Pet 3:18–19; CCC 632–33).

4:11 apostles . . . teachers: Ecclesial ministries associated with the proclamation of the Word. These positions are established to promote unity in the Church by (1) preserving doctrinal purity, (2) warding off false teaching (4:14), and (3) sanctifying people in truth (Jn 17:17–19). These spokesmen of the gospel build up the Body of Christ when they bring believers from immaturity to spiritual adulthood (4:15; CCC 1575, 2003–4). Other ministerial graces are listed in Rom 12:6–8 and 1 Cor 12:4–11. See note on 1 Cor 12:28.

4:15 speaking the truth: Or, "doing the truth". By bracing ourselves with the truth, we can resist the wind and waves of false teaching that unsettle the faith of immature believers. Paul is urging readers to grow in their knowledge of Christ (1:17; 4:23; Rom 12:2); otherwise their minds will remain childish, underdeveloped, and vulnerable to dangerous novelties that are contrary to the gospel (4:14). Here and elsewhere Paul insists that love is the surest means to build up the Church (4:16; 1 Cor 8:1; 13:1–13).

4:16 joined . . . growth: The same Greek verbs, which here describe the unity and growth of a body, also appear in 2:21, where they describe the integrated construction of a temple. The double use of this language in Ephesians points to a close connection between "body" and "temple" in Pauline theology (see also 1 Cor 6:19). This connection originates with Jesus, whose human body was the temple of his divinity (Jn 2:19–21). Applied to the living assembly of believers, it implies that the Church is a mystical extension of the Incarnation.

4:17 walk as the Gentiles walk: Believers must repudiate the behavior of pagans, whose minds are blind to gospel truth and whose wills are bent on evil rather than good. The same predicament of moral and intellectual depravity is outlined in Rom 1:18–32.

4:24 put on: Alludes to early liturgical practice in which catechumens were clothed in white robes immediately after Baptism. Metaphorically, Paul challenges us to put our baptismal commitments into practice by stripping off sinful habits (vices) and putting on the new garments of Christ (virtues) (Rom 13:14; Gal 3:27; CCC 1473).

The Four Marks of the Church

Of all the epistles of Paul, none speaks more eloquently or extensively of the Church than Ephesians. This unique letter outlines the essential characteristics of the Church, which the ancient creeds summarized as "one, holy, catholic, and apostolic". The Church is *one* because she has one source, the Blessed Trinity, and is unified in her faith, worship, and leadership. The Church is *holy* because Christ has separated her from sin and consecrated her to the Father. The Church is *catholic* because she bears within herself the fullness of grace and she embraces all nations. The Church is *apostolic* because she was founded upon the apostles, she preserves their apostolic doctrine, and she perpetuates a direct line of apostolic succession that stretches back to those first appointed by Christ. Paul touches directly or indirectly upon each of these marks in Ephesians.

The Church is **one**
"one Lord, one faith, one baptism"
(Eph 4:4)

The Church is **holy**
"that she might be holy and
without blemish"
(Eph 5:27)

The Church is **catholic**
"you [Gentiles] are fellow citizens with the
saints and members of the household of God"
(Eph 2:19)

The Church is **apostolic**
"built upon the foundation of the apostles
and prophets"
(Eph 2:20)

created after the likeness of God in true righteousness and holiness.

Rules for the New Life

25 Therefore, putting away falsehood, let every one speak the truth with his neighbor, for we are members one of another. [26]Be angry but do not sin; do not let the sun go down on your anger, [27]and give no opportunity to the devil. [28]Let the thief no longer steal, but rather let him labor, doing honest work with his hands, so that he may be able to give to those in need. [29]Let no evil talk come out of your mouths, but only such as is good for edifying, as fits the occasion, that it may impart grace to those who hear. [30]And do not grieve the Holy Spirit of God, in whom you were sealed for the day of redemption. [31]Let all bitterness and wrath and anger and clamor and slander be put away from you, with all malice, [32]and be kind to one another, tenderhearted, forgiving one another, as God in Christ forgave you.

5 Therefore be imitators of God, as beloved children. [2]And walk in love, as Christ loved us and gave himself up for us, a fragrant offering and sacrifice to God.

Renounce Pagan Ways

3 But immorality and all impurity or covetousness must not even be named among you, as is fitting among saints. [4]Let there be no filthiness, nor silly talk, nor levity, which are not fitting; but instead let there be thanksgiving. [5]Be sure of this, that no immoral or impure man, or one who is covetous (that is, an idolater), has any inheritance in the kingdom of Christ and of God. [6]Let no one deceive you with empty words, for it is because of these things that the wrath of God comes upon the sons of disobedience. [7]Therefore do not associate with them, [8]for once you were darkness, but now you are light in the Lord; walk as children of light [9](for the fruit of light is found in all that is good and right and true), [10]and try to learn what is pleasing to the Lord. [11]Take no part in the unfruitful works of darkness, but instead expose them. [12]For it is a shame even to speak of the things that they do in secret; [13]but when anything is exposed by the light it becomes visible, for anything that becomes visible is light. [14]Therefore it is said,

"Awake, O sleeper, and arise from the dead,
and Christ shall give you light."

15 Look carefully then how you walk, not as unwise men but as wise, [16]making the most of the time, because the days are evil. [17]Therefore do not be foolish, but understand what the will of the Lord is. [18]And do not get drunk with wine, for that

---

4:25: Zech 8:16; Rom 12:5. **5:2:** Ex 29:18; Ezek 20:41. **5:16:** Col 4:5.

4:25 putting away falsehood: Words should be spoken to help others and build them up, not to harm them or beat them down. Speech that is careless, slanderous, vulgar, or untruthful threatens the unity of the Church (4:29; Mt 12:36–37; Jas 3:1–12). The Lord despises a lying tongue (Prov 6:16–17) (CCC 2475–86). **speak the truth:** An excerpt from Zech 8:16. • The prophet is urging his people to reform their lives, beginning with a renewed effort to use truthful and reliable speech.

4:26 Be angry but do not sin: Not all anger is sinful or harmful. Righteous indignation is an appropriate response to offenses committed against God (Ps 119:53; Mk 3:5). In the case of personal insults, we should strive for reconciliation with the offender before the day's end. Otherwise the rift will begin to widen as resentment, bitterness, and hatred consume us. • Paul is alluding to Ps 4:4, where the Psalmist calls us to examine our hearts in silence before going to bed.

4:28 honest work: Generosity is urged as appropriate reparation for thievery. Reformed burglars should now work to provide for themselves as well as for others in need (Lk 3:11; Acts 20:35) (CCC 2444, 2487).

4:30 grieve the Holy Spirit: A warning to avoid sin and the occasions that lead to it. Paul is thinking primarily of destructive speech that disrupts unity and fellowship in the body of Christ (4:29, 31). Theologically, this comment confirms the "Personhood" of the Spirit, since only a person can be saddened or insulted by the faults of another. • Paul is alluding to Is 63:10, where the Prophet recalls how the Exodus generation of Israel grieved the Spirit by grumbling against the Lord and Moses in the wilderness. **day of redemption:** I.e., the day when our bodies will be redeemed at the general resurrection (Rom 8:23).

4:32 forgiving: We thank God for his mercy by showing mercy to others (Mt 6:14–15; 18:23–35; CCC 2842).

5:1 imitators of God: A challenge to love as God loves and to forgive as God has forgiven us (Mt 5:44–48; Lk 6:36; CCC 1694).

5:2 gave himself up: Jesus died as a priest who made his life a willing sacrifice. Paul explains this in cultic terms drawn from the OT. • Just as the priests of biblical history burned animals upon altars as a pleasing aroma to the Lord (Gen 8:20–21; Ex 29:18), so Jesus offered himself on the Cross as an ascending sacrifice of love to the Father (Heb 7:26–27; 10:8–10). We share in Christ's priestly ministry by offering to the Father acceptable sacrifices of our time, talents, and treasures in the liturgy of everyday life (Rom 12:1; 2 Cor 2:15) (CCC 614).

5:3 immorality: The Greek expression refers to fornication or sexual misconduct. Christians are forbidden to practice, think about, speak about, or even joke about such obscenities (5:4, 12). Christ has erected a high standard of chastity that restricts all sexual activity to the private quarters of lawful marriage (Heb 13:4).

5:5 an idolater: Any time we love and desire the world more than we love God, we make it an idol (Mt 6:24). The equation between covetousness and idolatry is also made in Col 3:5. **has any inheritance:** Sins of impurity are so grave that sexual offenders risk forfeiting heaven altogether. So unless the transgressor repents, he will perish with his illicit pleasures when "the wrath of God comes" at the Last Judgment (5:6). Notice that Paul is warning believers of this danger, implying that salvation, once attained, can still be lost (CCC 1861, 2351–59).

5:14 Awake, O sleeper: Possibly an excerpt from an ancient baptismal hymn. It resonates with the surrounding themes of light, symbolic of purity and truth, and darkness, symbolic of sin and ignorance (5:7–13). The summons to **arise from the dead** is a call to break away from the sinful world and live as children of light (5:7–8; 2 Cor 6:14) (CCC 1695).

5:16 making the most: Paul urges us to make prudent use of our time by seizing every opportunity to do good. Although we cannot lengthen time or add to our span of life, we can discipline ourselves to use our time more wisely and to fill it more fully (Col 4:5).

5:18 do not get drunk: Christians are called to live sober and respectable lives. For drunkenness opens the door to all kinds of dissipation (Prov 20:1), but sobriety enables

is debauchery; but be filled with the Spirit, ¹⁹addressing one another in psalms and hymns and spiritual songs, singing and making melody to the Lord with all your heart, ²⁰always and for everything giving thanks in the name of our Lord Jesus Christ to God the Father.

The Christian Household

21 Be subject to one another out of reverence for Christ. ²²Wives, be subject to your husbands, as to the Lord. ²³For the husband is the head of the wife as Christ is the head of the Church, his body, and is himself its Savior. ²⁴As the Church is subject to Christ, so let wives also be subject in everything to

their husbands. ²⁵Husbands, love your wives, as Christ loved the Church and gave himself up for her, ²⁶that he might sanctify her, having cleansed her by the washing of water with the word, ²⁷that he might present the Church to himself in splendor, without spot or wrinkle or any such thing, that she might be holy and without blemish. ²⁸Even so husbands should love their wives as their own bodies. He who loves his wife loves himself. ²⁹For no man ever hates his own flesh, but nourishes and cherishes it, as Christ does the Church, ³⁰because we are members of his body. ³¹"For this reason a man shall leave his father and mother and be joined to his

---

5:19: Col 3:16–17. **5:22–6:9:** Col 3:18—4:1.

---

us to live under the influence of the Spirit (Rom 8:5–11). Note that Paul advocates temperance and not strict abstinence from alcohol (1 Tim 5:23; CCC 1809). ● The command is taken from the Greek version of Prov 23:31.

5:21 subject to one another: This verse marks a transition into Paul's teaching on family life. He calls for mutual submission within the network of relationships that follow: husbands and wives (5:22–25), parents and children (6:1–4), slaves and masters (6:5–9). The submission Paul enjoins in these various circumstances is reciprocal although not strictly identical, for the commands given to husbands, fathers, and masters are different from those given to wives, children, and slaves. For similar household codes, see Col 3:18—4:1 and 1 Pet 2:13—3:12 (CCC 1642).

5:22–33 Paul views Christian marriage through the lens of Christ's covenant love for the Church. This analogy of faith highlights (1) the *indissolubility* of Christian marriage, since Christ will never withdraw from the Church or disown her, (2) the *sacramentality* of Christian marriage, since marital love is a living sign of Christ's love for the Church, and (3) the *reciprocity* of Christian marriage, since the Church submits to Christ's leadership even as Christ the bridegroom acquiesces to the prayers of his beloved bride. ● The marital union between Christ and the Church in the New Covenant (2 Cor 11:2; Rev 19:7-9) recalls the marriage covenant between Yahweh and Israel in the Old Covenant (Is 54:5-8; Hos 2:16-20) (CCC 1612, 1641).

5:22 Wives, be subject: The Greek implies her submission is free and voluntary, not degrading, servile, or coercive (Col 3:18; Tit 2:5; 1 Pet 3:1). Since a wife entrusts herself to her husband as part of her devotion to the Lord, her submission cannot be unconditional, especially if her husband commands what God expressly forbids (Acts 5:29). Though ancient society often viewed wives as the property of their husbands, Paul sees marriage as a loving partnership between spouses of equal dignity (Gal 3:28).

5:25 Husbands, love: The husband's mission is to build up his marriage and family, not to dominate or demean them for selfish ends. His model is Christ, whose love was put into action by sacrifice. Again, Paul confronts prevailing customs, where husbands often reigned like tyrants over their household (Col 3:19; 1 Pet 3:7).

5:26 washing of water: A reference to Baptism, which cleanses the soul of sin and beautifies it with grace (Acts 22:16; 1 Cor 6:11; Tit 3:5). The accompanying **word** refers to the baptismal formula spoken as the sacrament is administered (Mt 28:19) or possibly to the cleansing power of the gospel (Jn 15:3). According to Jewish marital custom, brides were presented to their bridegrooms after bathing and adorning themselves (CCC 1228). ● Paul's comments recall the symbolic imagery of Ezek 16:8-14, where Yahweh entered a covenant of marriage with Jerusalem after bathing her in water and clothing her with beautiful garments. In the new economy, Christ weds the Church to himself after cleansing her in Baptism and

clothing her with the fine linen of righteous deeds (Rev 19:7-8) (CCC 1617).

5:27 without spot or wrinkle: Evokes the image of a garment that is clean and pressed.

5:29 nourishes: The concern of a husband to meet his physical needs should likewise bring him to cherish his wife. ● The close connection drawn between a man's flesh and a man's wife stems from Genesis, where the Lord used Adam's own flesh and bone to form his bride, Eve (Gen 2:21-23). ● Paul's allusion to Adam and Eve implies a greater truth about Christ. He, too, fashions his bride, the Church, by giving her the sacramental substance of his own flesh and blood in the Eucharist. This is what makes the Church his **own flesh** (CCC 757, 1003). See note on Jn 19:34.

5:31 two shall become one: A citation from Gen 2:24. ● Genesis recounts the institution of marriage, between

---

Word Study

Head (Eph 5:23)

Kephalē (Gk.): "head". The term is found 75 times in the NT and numerous times in the Greek OT. It can refer to the physical "head" of a man (Mt 5:36), animal (Gen 3:15), or statue (Dan 2:32). It can also mean "ruler" or "leader", as when King David is called the head of the nations (Ps 18:43) and when Christ is called the head of all things (Eph 1:22). Other ancient texts attest the meaning "source" or "origin", as when Herodotus refers to the headwaters of a river (*Histories* 4, 91), when the Jewish philosopher Philo describes Esau as the progenitor of his entire clan (*On the Preliminary Studies* 12, 61), and when the Jewish author of the Testaments of the Twelve Patriarchs identifies deceitful spirits as the source of youthful misbehavior (*Testament of Reuben* 2, 2). Paul uses this term in his teaching on marriage to encourage husbands to be heads or leaders within the home as Christ is head over the Church (1 Cor 11:3; Eph 5:23). As the context of these passages shows, Paul views marital headship through the creation narratives of Genesis, where Adam was both the head and source of his wife, Eve (Gen 2:21-23), just as Christ is the head and source of the Church (Eph 4:15–16; Col 2:19). For Paul, then, the Body of Christ can be pictured as the *torso* of Christ (anatomical image) as well as the *bride* of Christ (marital image). For more on this Pauline theme, see note on 1 Cor 12:21.

wife, and the two shall become one flesh." [32]This is a great mystery, and I mean in reference to Christ and the Church; [33]however, let each one of you love his wife as himself, and let the wife see that she respects her husband.

Children and Parents

6 Children, obey your parents in the Lord, for this is right. [2]"Honor your father and mother" (this is the first commandment with a promise), [3]"that it may be well with you and that you may live long on the earth." [4]Fathers, do not provoke your children to anger, but bring them up in the discipline and instruction of the Lord.

Slaves and Masters

5 Slaves, be obedient to those who are your earthly masters, with fear and trembling, in singleness of heart, as to Christ; [6]not in the way of eyeservice, as men-pleasers, but as servants [f] of Christ, doing the will of God from the heart, [7]rendering service with a good will as to the Lord and not to men, [8]knowing that whatever good any one does, he will receive the same again from the Lord, whether he is a slave or free. [9]Masters, do the same to them, and forbear threatening, knowing that he who is both their Master and yours is in heaven, and that there is no partiality with him.

The Whole Armor of God

10 Finally, be strong in the Lord and in the strength of his might. [11]Put on the whole armor of God, that you may be able to stand against the wiles of the devil. [12]For we are not contending against flesh and blood, but against the principalities, against the powers, against the world rulers of this present darkness, against the spiritual hosts of wickedness in the heavenly places. [13]Therefore take the whole armor of God, that you may be able to withstand in the evil day, and having done all, to stand. [14]Stand therefore, having fastened the belt of truth around your waist, and having put on the breastplate of righteousness, [15]and having shod your feet with the equipment of the gospel of peace; [16]besides all these, taking the shield of faith, with which you can quench all the flaming darts of the Evil One. [17]And take the helmet of salvation, and the sword of the Spirit, which is the word of God. [18]Pray at all times in the Spirit, with all prayer and

---

5:31: Gen 2:24.   6:2: Ex 20:12.   6:3: Deut 5:16.   6:14: Is 11:5; 59:17; 1 Thess 5:8.   6:15: Is 52:7.

---

the first couple, Adam and Eve. Despite God's intention that this covenant be a permanent, fruitful, and exclusive bond of companionship, numerous deviations from the divine plan have marred its beauty over the centuries (e.g., polygamy, divorce, adultery, concubinage). Christ came to redeem marriage from these aberrations, restore its original dignity, and enrich it with sacramental grace (Mt 19:3-9) (CCC 1605, 1615-16).

5:32 mystery: Marriage is an earthly image of the heavenly union between Christ and the Church. This spiritual symbolism was hidden from the beginning in the marital covenant and is now manifest in the New Covenant. Saint Jerome rendered the Greek word for "mystery" as *sacramentum* (sacrament) in the original Latin Vulgate (CCC 774-76). See word study: *Mystery* at Eph 3:3.

6:2 Honor your father and mother: A citation from Deut 5:16. • This is the fourth commandment of the Decalogue and the first of the ten directed toward loving our neighbor (CCC 2214-18). It comes with a blessing of happiness and longevity (6:3) for those who obey their parents and care for them in old age (Sir 3:1-16). Rebellion against parental authority was commonplace among the pagans (Rom 1:30) and a capital offense in ancient Israel (Ex 21:17; Deut 21:18-21).

6:4 Fathers, do not provoke: A warning not to discourage children by unreasonable discipline or restraint (Col 3:21). Parents must instead take responsibility for the moral (**discipline**) and intellectual formation (**instruction**) of their children in accordance with the gospel. Just as parents provide their children's bodies with food, clothing, and shelter, so they must nourish their children's souls with loving correction and Christian truth (Deut 6:6-7; Prov 13:24; Heb 12:7-11) (CCC 2221-30).

6:5 Slaves, be obedient: Slavery was widely accepted in the ancient world and was often cruel and inhumane. For this reason, Paul stresses the equal dignity of slaves and their masters before God (6:8) and seeks to improve the relationship between them (6:9). Slaves are summoned to serve their masters willingly and honestly, while masters are called to respect their servants and refrain from harsh treatment. Although Paul does not challenge the institution of slavery directly, the principles of his gospel work indirectly against it (Gal 3:28; Philem 16). See note on 1 Cor 7:21.

6:10-17 Paul warns readers of the spiritual warfare that rages unseen in the Church. For Christ's kingdom does not spread free of opposition or enemies; rather, it is daily attacked by malevolent spirits under the command of Satan. Our first defense is the **armor of God**, i.e., the graces given to protect us in times of temptation. Our weaponry is both offensive (sword) and defensive (breastplate, shield, helmet, protective footwear), enabling us to ward off the powers of darkness and to guard ourselves from exposure to their tactics (2 Cor 6:7; 10:3-5; 1 Thess 5:8). Although the devil and his demons were defeated by Christ on the Cross (Col 2:15), they remain dangerous until he comes again to destroy them (1 Cor 15:24-25; Rev 20:10). • Paul alludes to Wis 5:17-20 and Is 59:17. Both passages depict Yahweh as a warrior suiting up for battle against the ungodly. The Church joins him in this holy war as believers are enlisted among his troops and equipped with his divine armory. This OT background suggests that Paul's imagery is more closely linked with Yahweh's spiritual armor than with the military gear of a Roman soldier. • To put on the armor of God is to put on the Lord Jesus Christ. Called truth and righteousness, our Savior is our belt and our breastplate. Called the living Word of God, he is the sword who is sharp on both sides (St. Jerome, *Commentary on Ephesians* 3, 6).

6:12 flesh and blood: A Semitic idiom for what is merely human (Mt 16:17; 1 Cor 15:50). **principalities . . . powers . . . rulers:** Ranks of demonic spirits opposed to the Church. See note on 1:21.

6:15 your feet . . . gospel of peace: An allusion to Is 52:7. • Isaiah envisions Yahweh reigning on Mt. Zion after crushing his enemies and redeeming his people. News of his victory travels on foot as messengers bring "good tidings" of "peace" and "salvation" to the ends of the earth. Paul sees this prophecy unfolding in the lives of believers as they carry the gospel to the world. It is assumed that the steady advance of God's kingdom means the steady retreat of all opposing forces.

6:18 Pray at all times: A command closely linked with Paul's preceding instruction on spiritual warfare (CCC 2633, 2742). It indicates that our perseverance in prayer must match the relentless persistence of the devil (Lk 18:1; 1 Thess 5:17). We can expect no truce between God's family and God's enemies before the Day of Judgment (2 Pet 2:4).

---

[f] Or *slaves*.

supplication. To that end keep alert with all perseverance, making supplication for all the saints, [19]and also for me, that utterance may be given me in opening my mouth boldly to proclaim the mystery of the gospel, [20]for which I am an ambassador in chains; that I may declare it boldly, as I ought to speak.

Personal Matters and Benediction

21 Now that you also may know how I am and what I am doing, Tych'icus the beloved brother and faithful minister in the Lord will tell you everything. [22]I have sent him to you for this very purpose, that you may know how we are, and that he may encourage your hearts.

23 Peace be to the brethren, and love with faith, from God the Father and the Lord Jesus Christ. [24]Grace be with all who love our Lord Jesus Christ with love undying.

6:21–22: Col 4:7–8.

6:20 ambassador in chains: Paul is likely writing as a prisoner under house arrest in Rome (Acts 28:16), where he was given freedom to preach to the crowds who came to him (Acts 28:23–31). This would explain why he asks readers to pray on his behalf for the grace of evangelical boldness (6:19).

6:21 Tychicus: The courier Paul assigned to deliver this letter as well as Colossians (Col 4:7–8). If he is the same person from "Asia" mentioned in Acts 20:4, he would already be familiar with the cities of Ephesus and Colossae in Asia Minor (southwest Turkey).

STUDY QUESTIONS

Ephesians

Chapter 1

For understanding
1. **1:3–14.** How does Paul open this letter? What is his principle of organization? What is significant about the blessings that Paul celebrates? What Jewish prayer form does Paul's blessing follow?
2. **1:5.** For what has the Father predestined believers? Which two mysteries does the doctrine of predestination hold together? What can we *not* know about in regard to predestination, and what can we indeed know? What was God unconcerned about when he predestined us?
3. **Word Study: Unite (1:10).** What does the rarely used Greek word for "recapitulate" or "sum up under one head" refer to in normal usage? How does Paul use this Greek word in Rom 13:9? in this verse? How do the figures of Adam and Christ form the background of Paul's idea?
4. **1:21.** To what does the expression "rule and authority and power" refer here? What point is Paul making? What are the nine "choirs" of angels recognized by Catholic theologians, and how are they arranged?

For application
1. **1:9.** How aware are you of the mystery behind the ways you think or make choices or even of who you are? For example, how well do you understand yourself? What does it mean for you that God's will—which Paul says is made known to us—even so remains a mystery?
2. **1:13.** Since you "have heard the word of truth, the gospel of your salvation", how would you show that you actually believe it? How seriously do you take your Confirmation?
3. **1:17.** What does "knowledge" of God mean? How does Paul pray that you will acquire it?
4. **1:19.** Paul refers to the "immeasurable greatness of his power in us who believe". What is that power? How have you experienced it *as power* in your life? If you do not experience spiritual power, what do you need to do to receive it?

Chapter 2

For understanding
1. **2:8.** To what does the word *grace* refer, here? What does each meaning designate? What is the meaning of salvation in this context?
2. **2:10.** What works are made possible by the grace of God within us? What did the Second Council of Orange teach in A.D. 529 about grace and good works?
3. **2:14.** What is the dividing wall that Paul is thinking of in this verse, and what does it symbolize? What has Christ done to it?
4. **2:20.** What symbolic architectural role do the apostles and prophets play in the Church? What is the role of a cornerstone, and how does it apply to Christ? How does Jewish tradition treat the idea of a cornerstone?

For application
1. **2:1–2.** What characteristic behavior might a person show who is physically alive but spiritually dead? Though Paul does not specify here what "trespasses and sins" would cause spiritual death, which of them pose the greatest threat to you? What are "sons of disobedience", and what spirit do they follow?
2. **2:4–10.** What do these verses have to say to those who feel unworthy of God's consideration or that their sins are unforgivable?
3. **2:14–16.** Within your family—whether immediate or extended—how might Christ bring peace where there might have been feuds, long-term disagreements, or strained relationships? What should your own role be in bringing that peace to bear on such problems?
4. **2:19–22.** How would you characterize your relationship with the Catholic Church? Do you see yourself as a spiritual nobody or as a fellow citizen with all the saints? Alternatively, do you regard yourself as a stranger just passing through or as a member of the household? How might you change from being a nobody or a passerby to a family member?

Chapter 3

For understanding
1. **Word Study: Mystery (3:3).** When Paul uses the term *mystery*, what is he teaching about? What is the OT background of this notion? How does Daniel's use of "mystery" apply to what Paul is teaching?
2. **3:14.** What is the significance of "bowing the knee"? What does it express?
3. **3:15.** To what kind of grouping does the Greek word for *family* refer? How does that meaning apply to the family role of God?
4. **3:18.** To what do the dimensions listed here refer? What are some other possibilities? How did St. Gregory of Nyssa understand these terms?

For application
1. **3:4–6.** From whom did you "inherit" your faith? Why are you a Christian and not a member of some other religion? What appreciation do you have for the value of this inheritance?
2. **3:8.** Where would you rank yourself among the saints? By what standard would you rank yourself at all? In comparison with the grace Paul claims for himself here, what grace would you claim God has given you for the benefit of others?
3. **3:14–19.** How would you apply Paul's prayer to yourself? What kind of inner strength do you most need? What does it mean to be "rooted and grounded in love"? Of what kind of power do vv. 18 and 19 speak?
4. **3:20–21.** What are some of the limits you set yourself for the things you can "ask or think" in your relationship with the Father? What do you *avoid* asking for? How might praise of the Father expand those limits?

Chapter 4

For understanding
1. **Chart: The Four Marks of the Church (Eph 4).** In Ephesians, how does Paul touch upon the four essential characteristics of the Church? What does he understand them to mean? What specific verses refer to each of the four marks?
2. **4:11.** What are the ecclesial ministries listed by Paul in this verse established to promote, and how?
3. **4:26.** What is an example of anger that is an appropriate response? When insulted, why should we strive for reconciliation before the day's end? To which psalm is Paul alluding?
4. **4:30.** By warning us not to "grieve the Holy Spirit", of what is Paul primarily thinking? What do his words confirm about the Holy Spirit? What does Isaiah 63 (to which Paul here alludes) mention as having grieved the Spirit?

For application
1. **4:15.** According to Paul, how should you speak the truth to others? How does love "improve" the truth of what you say? What are some other ways you can speak the truth to others, and what are the likely consequences of speaking it in those ways?
2. **4:17–24.** According to Paul, what causes the mental futility, darkened understanding, and alienation of our pagan society? To what types of behavior does it lead? What might be the effects of the change he proposes in the last three verses?
3. **4:25.** Compare this verse with v. 15. What is the motive he gives in each verse for telling the truth? As you read from here to the end of chapter 4, what kind of emphasis is Paul placing on truthful speech?
4. **4:29.** What are some of your negative speech habits? For example, how habitually do you speak in a way that criticizes or labels others, especially those to whom you are close? If you were typically to speak to them in an edifying way, how "natural" do you think such a speech habit would feel to you at first? in the long run?

Chapter 5

For understanding
1. **5:22–33.** How does Paul view Christian marriage in these verses? What three aspects of marriage does this analogy of faith highlight? What Old Covenant relationship does the marital union between Christ and the Church recall?
2. **5:22.** What does the Greek imply about the submission of the wife? What are the limits of that submission? What is the difference between the perspective of Paul and that of ancient society?
3. **Word Study: Head (5:23).** How is the term "head" used in the Bible? How do non-biblical writers of antiquity use the term? How does Paul use the term in reference to husbands? How does he use Genesis in his thinking, and what reference does it have to Christ?
4. **5:26.** To what sacrament is Paul alluding here? To what might the term *word* refer? How were Jewish brides prepared for presentation to their grooms? What OT imagery stands in the background?

For application
1. **5:8–13.** What kinds of behavior or activities do you keep secret from friends or relatives or try to explain away? Which do you let others see or are proud of? Which class of behavior best fits the standard of v. 9?
2. **5:18–20.** How might following Paul's recommendations make a difference in the way you speak and even pray?
3. **5:21–24.** Look up paragraph 1605 in the *Catechism of the Catholic Church*: What is the meaning that the *Catechism* attaches to the word "helpmate"? How should the wife relate to the husband? For that matter, how should anyone (male or female) relate to Christ?
4. **5:25.** How is the husband to love his wife? To what (implied) extent?

Chapter 6

For understanding
1. **6:2.** Which commandment is Paul quoting, and what is its OT source? What blessing accompanies it? How seriously did ancient Israel treat rebellion against parental authority?
2. **6:5.** What is the difference between the usual treatment of slaves and Paul's view of slavery? What are the reciprocal duties of Christian slaves and Christian masters?
3. **6:10–17.** What is the "armor of God" we need in order to resist the daily attacks by malevolent spirits? In Paul's inventory, what kinds of weapons do we have? How do the OT books of Wisdom and Isaiah, to which Paul alludes, picture Yahweh? What does this OT background suggest for our reading of the passage?
4. **6:18.** What does Paul's command to "pray at all times" indicate for us? What can we expect in our spiritual warfare?

For application
1. **6:1–4.** If you are a parent, how do you discipline your children? What forms of praise and punishment do you use? Which of these seems to predominate?
2. **6:5–9.** If you are an employee, how would you apply vv. 5–8 to yourself? If you are an employer, a manager, or a supervisor, how might your management style be affected by applying v. 9 to your subordinates?
3. **6:12–13.** Do you believe in the reality of spiritual warfare? How have you experienced its reality in your own life? What is going on now that you might call spiritual warfare? If you do not believe that events—especially negative ones—reflect "warfare" of a spiritual nature, how would you explain what Paul is talking about?
4. **6:18.** In what ways do you engage in intercessory prayer? For whom do you pray? For whom might you be neglecting to pray, and what will you do about it?

BOOKS OF THE BIBLE

THE OLD TESTAMENT

Gen	Genesis
Ex	Exodus
Lev	Leviticus
Num	Numbers
Deut	Deuteronomy
Josh	Joshua
Judg	Judges
Ruth	Ruth
1 Sam	1 Samuel
2 Sam	2 Samuel
1 Kings	1 Kings
2 Kings	2 Kings
1 Chron	1 Chronicles
2 Chron	2 Chronicles
Ezra	Ezra
Neh	Nehemiah
Tob	Tobit
Jud	Judith
Esther	Esther
Job	Job
Ps	Psalms
Prov	Proverbs
Eccles	Ecclesiastes
Song	Song of Solomon
Wis	Wisdom
Sir	Sirach (Ecclesiasticus)
Is	Isaiah
Jer	Jeremiah
Lam	Lamentations
Bar	Baruch
Ezek	Ezekiel
Dan	Daniel
Hos	Hosea
Joel	Joel
Amos	Amos
Obad	Obadiah
Jon	Jonah
Mic	Micah
Nahum	Nahum
Hab	Habakkuk
Zeph	Zephaniah
Hag	Haggai
Zech	Zechariah
Mal	Malachi
1 Mac	1 Maccabees
2 Mac	2 Maccabees

THE NEW TESTAMENT

Mt	Matthew
Mk	Mark
Lk	Luke
Jn	John
Acts	Acts of the Apostles
Rom	Romans
1 Cor	1 Corinthians
2 Cor	2 Corinthians
Gal	Galatians
Eph	Ephesians
Phil	Philippians
Col	Colossians
1 Thess	1 Thessalonians
2 Thess	2 Thessalonians
1 Tim	1 Timothy
2 Tim	2 Timothy
Tit	Titus
Philem	Philemon
Heb	Hebrews
Jas	James
1 Pet	1 Peter
2 Pet	2 Peter
1 Jn	1 John
2 Jn	2 John
3 Jn	3 John
Jude	Jude
Rev	Revelation (Apocalypse)

NOTES

NOTES

NOTES